PARACHUTE PLAY

By
Liz & Dick Wilmes
Art
Jeane Healy

A BUILDING BLOCKS Publication

3893 Brindlewood, Elgin, Illinois 60120

ISBN 0-943452-03-1
Library of Congress Catalog No. 85-071415

COVER CONSULTANTS:
Pat and Greg Samata
Samata Associates, Inc.
Dundee, Illinois

About the illustrator:
Jeane Healy is a free lance artist who specializes in the early childhood field. During the last eight years, Jeane has been sharing her talent and expertise with the readers of Building Blocks Newspaper, Everyday Circle Times and now Parachute Play. In addition Jeane's illustrations have appeared in Mother Earth and Mothering magazines to name a few.
She lives in Elgin with her husband Steve and two daughters, Devon and Molly.

PUBLISHED BY:
BUILDING BLOCKS
3893 Brindlewood
Elgin, Illinois 60120

DISTRIBUTED BY:
GRYPHON HOUSE, Inc.
P.O. Box 275
Mt. Rainier, Maryland 20712

ISBN 0-943452-03-1
>> $7.95

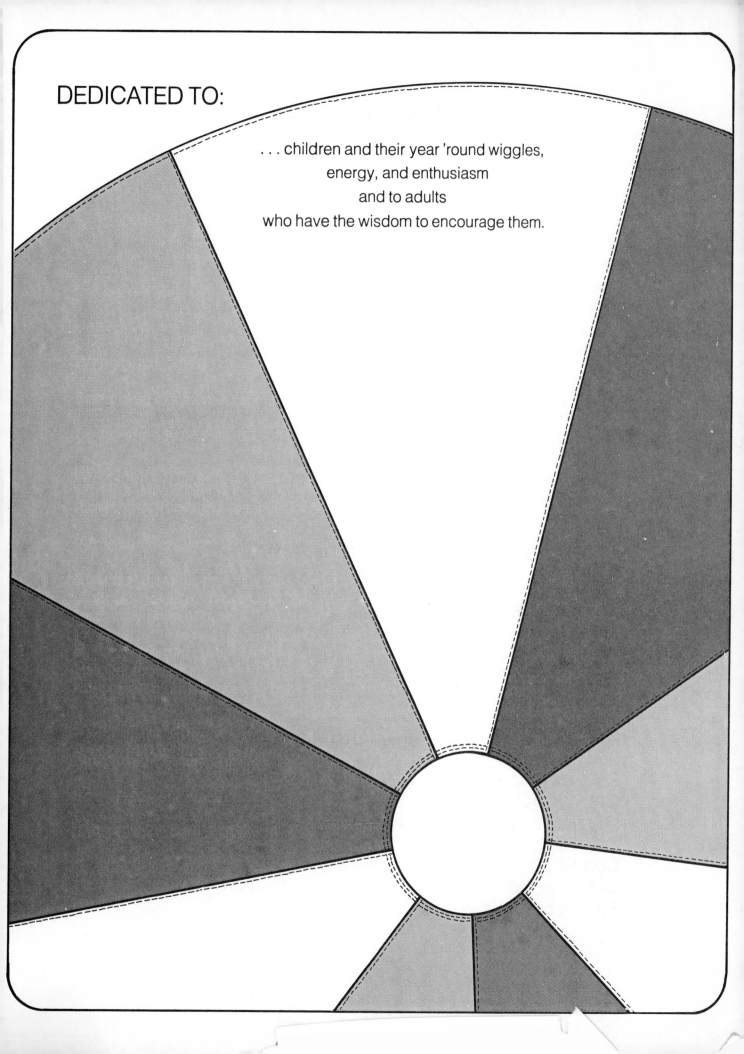

DEDICATED TO:

. . . children and their year 'round wiggles,
energy, and enthusiasm
and to adults
who have the wisdom to encourage them.

Contents

Dedication 3

Introduction
Why Parachute Play? 6
Using Parachute Play 6
Keeping Things Under Control 7

At A Glance 9

Eight Basic Sessions
Session 1 17
Session 2 21
Session 3 23
Session 4 26
Session 5 30
Session 6 33
Session 7 36
Session 8 39

Year 'Round Activities
Around the Chute 44
Up and Down 45
Going to the Zoo 47
Pop Flies 48
Scarf Dancing 49
Move Quickly 51
Bounce the Ball 52
Build an Igloo 53
Grab the Beanbag 55
Wiggle Worm 56
Say "Hi" 57
Cool Off 59
Catch the Ball 60
Parachute Catch 61

Year 'Round Activities (cont.)

Floating the Chute 63
Body Parts 64
Kite Flying 65
Floating Clouds 67
Parachute Golf 68
Tag 69
Bug In My Chute 70
Row Your Boat 71

Holiday Activities

Happy New Year 74
Ice Skating 74
Heart Match 75
Shadows 76
Who Is Patrick? 77
Bunny Hop 78
Colored Egg Hunt 79
Maypole March 80
Where Are the Bees? 81
Old Glory 82
Tug, Tug, Tug 83
Dunk Tank 83
Happy Birthday 84
How Old Are You? 84
Old McDonald Had A Farm 85
Apple Seed 86
Haunted House 87
Run Fast Little Turkey 88
Pass the Hat 89
Find Your Shoes 90
Jingle Bells 90
Wrapping Gifts 91
Snow Angels 91

Introduction

Why Parachute Play?

Parachutes are one of the most versatile pieces of equipment that you can use with young children. Through the wide variety of activities you are able to enjoy with the chute, children will increase their ability to:
- Follow directions.
- Use language.
- Join group activities.
- Socialize.
- Develop small muscle control.
- Strengthen large muscles.
- Remain in control during very active play.

Using Parachute Play

PARACHUTE PLAY is divided into three sections: the eight basic sessions, the year 'round activities, and the special holiday activities.

It is very important that you do the basic sessions with the children before you enjoy any of the other exercises and/or activities in PARACHUTE PLAY. Each of the eight sessions is designed for ten to fifteen minutes of parachute fun. This is enough time to learn new skills, have fun, and not get too tired.

After enjoying a wide variety of simple activities in these sessions, the children will have:
- Learned different ways to hold and move the chute.
- Developed more strength.
- Learned how to control balls on the parachute.
- Experienced going under the chute.
- Developed an understanding of group games.
- Developed the discipline to enjoy the more active and slightly longer activities described in the other two sections.

Children and adults need time to learn and to understand how the parachute reacts when they move it in different ways. The children must also feel confident that they can control the chute and make it do what they want it to do. By going through the first eight sessions in a slightly structured manner, everyone will learn the skills they need to enjoy the endless variety of games, activities, and exercises described in PARACHUTE PLAY.

Part II is a compilation of parachute exercises, games and activities that young children can enjoy anytime during the year. Each activity begins with a warm-up exercise done with the chute, followed by the main activity, and ending with a quiet resting type game. All of the exercises, games, and activities use and build upon the skills which were introduced in the beginning eight sessions. Parachute play is ongoing fun. Each time you and the children use the chute, you will all learn more about it, laugh, and get rid of your excess wiggles.

Part III is a specially developed section of activities designed to add a little more fun and frolic to each major holiday and season. Divided into twelve months, the activities expand the versatility of the chute by introducing music, suggesting more accessories such as streamers, balloons, and bells, and converting the chute to such fun things as the ground hog's hole, a giant birthday cake, a haunted house, or an ice skating pond.

Keeping Things Under Control

People often think that parachute play is a 'wild' and 'uncontrolled' activity. Parachute play can be and should be a controlled, very active, and really fun type of activity.

When you're doing parachute play, keep several things in mind. They will all help you and the children enjoy your parachute play more.

- Start and end every activity with the parachute in a bunched up position.
- Use the *"STOP"* direction to control the flow of every activity.
- Always take time to rest during and between activities as children tire. Use these rest periods to talk about how the parachute looks and feels. Is it making noise? What body parts are the children using in that particular activity?
- Use slow, quiet activities to bring children from an excited, fast-paced state to a more relaxed condition.
- Vary the suggested exercises and activities by changing body positions, hand grips, parachute positions, and parachute motions.

 # AT A GLANCE

Parachute Grips

There are four basic ways to grip the parachute. Children should learn to use the first two grips before they are introduced to the last two.

Thumbs-Up: In this grip the fingers are under the parachute and the thumbs are visible over the chute. In other words, the fists are holding onto the parachute underneath it and the thumbs are up, holding onto parachute material from above.

Thumbs-Down: This grip is the opposite of Thumbs-Up. The thumbs are holding the parachute underneath and the four fingers are visible over the parachute. Thus, in this grip, the fingers are up and the thumbs are down.

Thumb-Up - Thumb-Down: As was stated above, this grip is more difficult and should be used for variety after the children are comfortable with the first two grips. To do this grip, the children grab the parachute using the Thumbs-Up grip with one hand the Thumbs-Down grip with the other one.

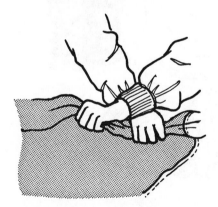

Arms-Crossed: This grip is another variation of the first two grips and can be used for diversity in many of the activities. The children should cross their arms over each other and grab the parachute with either the Thumbs-Up or Thumbs-Down grip.

In addition to using one of the four grips, the children must learn to firmly hold the parachute. To do this they first need to grab a handful of the parachute material. This is difficult in the beginning because their hands are small, their muscles are not very strong, and parachute material is slippery. Secondly, the children should remember to keep their fists closed. Again this is hard in the beginning because their hands easily get tired and because they get so involved with the activity they forget to hold on and consequently the parachute gets jerked out of their hands.

Body Positions

Many parachute games can be done from all three body positions. Depending on the activity, there is usually a best or most comfortable position from which to enjoy each game. Start with that position and then do the activity again from one of the other two positions. After you have tried it from at least two different body positions, talk about the two approaches. See if the children felt any differences.

- **Sitting With the Parachute:** Though there are many ways to sit on the floor, cross-legged is the most appropriate for the majority of parachute activities. For some games, the children will, however, sit with their legs straight out.

    Using the sitting position is the least active of all of the positions, because the chidren are most limited in their movements and a minimal amount of air is trapped under the parachute. As you will soon discover, sitting is usually the least fun and not used as often as kneeling and standing.

    It is, however, a great position from which to teach most activities. The children are more able to concentrate on the directions from a sitting position than they are from a kneeling or standing one.

- **Kneeling With the Parachute:** As with the sitting position, the kneeling position is a great one from which to teach a new activity or vary an old one. Because the parachute is higher off of the ground than in the sitting position, more air is trapped under the chute to get a fuller, higher effect from the parachute movements. Because the children are on their knees, they can move more freely.

- **Standing With the Parachute:** As you and your group of children feel more and more comfortable with parachute play, you will discover that you do many of the activities from a standing position and use the sitting and kneeling positions for the variations.

    To fully enjoy any activity from this position be sure that the children understand the directions. If you find that they do not, switch to one of the other positions and do the activity from there.

    In the standing position, the greatest amount of air is under the parachute and the children are able to move freely in many ways.

Parachute Positions

Though the parachute can be held in any position in relationship to the body, there are generally three places from which most parachute activities originate. For each game, there is usually a most appropriate position and the other two are used for variation and added excitement or challenge when you repeat the games. Other times, more than one position is used during a game. The activity may begin in a certain place and switch to another position depending on the flow of the activity.

    Because of the constant movement of the parachute, the children must be very familiar with the three main positions and how it feels to hold the parachute in each of them.

- **Way Up High:** When holding the parachute in this position, children extend their arms over their heads so the parachute is floating above the group. Though this is a really fun and an exciting way to hold the parachute, it is also the most tiring. During activities which use this position, you must have many opportunities to rest throughout the flow of the game. The more the children use the parachute, the stronger they will become and their need for rest breaks diminish. Use the rest period to talk about what is happening to the parachute and how the children feel.

- **Way Down Low:** When the children hold the parachute low, it usually floats around their knees. If it floats much lower than that, you will not get enough air under the parachute to get the effects you want. Doing activities with the parachute in this position is usually very quieting for the children. It is great to use this position while doing the last activity or variation in the sequence. By using it, the children will most often finish the parachute play in a calm manner and be able to transition to the next activity of the day with no excess energy.

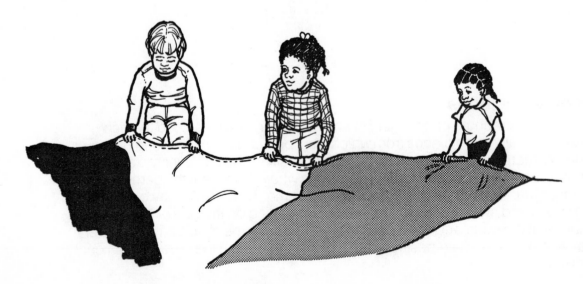

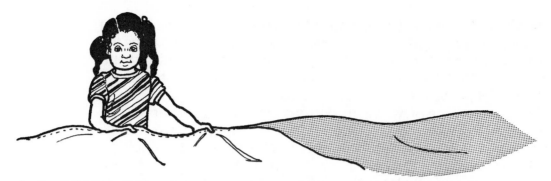

- **In the Middle:** Of the three parachute positions this one is used the most and is the most comfortable to maintain. The parachute is held right around the waist. From there, children can enjoy many of the activities as well as easily move the parachute to a higher or lower position.

Other than the three basic parachute positions used for the activities, there is also the resting position. Parachute play can be very active. As you enjoy the different games, you will need to periodically take a break. During rest times, continue to hold onto the parachute (unless otherwise instructed) whether you are sitting, kneeling, or standing. Usually it is most relaxing if the children simply let their arms hang loosely in front of them.

Parachute Motions

By moving their arms, hands, and wrists in different combinations, a group of people can make a parachute wiggle in a variety of ways. The different effects which are created are used in various parachute activities. There are four basic movements. Enjoy these first and then create variations and new motions.

13

- **The Wave:** There are two types of waving motions. The first one is a simple both arms up-both arms down motion. Each person does this up and down motion as an individual. He does not do it in unison with the group. This type of movement causes a shallow rippling effect in the chute. It is a very basic motion and used often.

    The second type of waving motion is once again a both arms up-both arms down movement, but this time the group must do it in unison, that is, everyone up-everyone down. Instead of the rippling effect caused by the first type of waving motion, the parachute billows high in the air and creates a giant wave. This second type of waving motion is more spectacular than the first and requires more control of the parachute.

- **The Jerk:** The jerk is a side to side movement of the parachute. Hold the parachute with two hands. You can do this movement in rhythm with everyone jerking right and left, continuing right-left, right-left, right-left. You can also do this movement more randomly with each person individually jerking right and left. The type of parachute game you play will dictate which type of jerk you'll use.

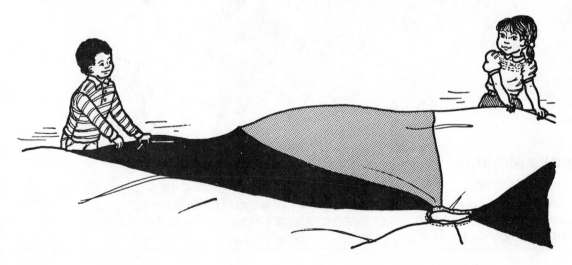

- **The Flip-Flop:** In the waving motion everyone moves both of his arms up and then both down. In the flip-flop each person alternates his arms, so that when the right arm is up, the left one is down. When doing the flip-flop the parachute wiggles and jiggles randomly. It is one of the children's favorites, especially when doing it very quickly.

- **Taut:** When holding the parachute taut, everyone pulls back on the chute until it is completely spread out and has no slack in it. The type of exercise or activity you are going to play will dictate how hard you will pull on the parachute. In the beginning young children will only be able to pull slightly. As they learn how to hold onto the chute tightly and have more strength they will be able to pull the chute more taut.

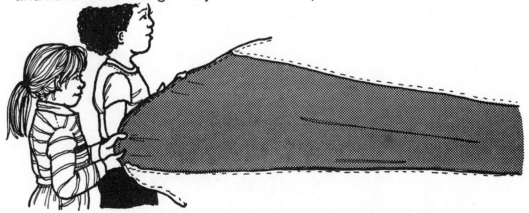

- **The Snap:** The snap is probably the most difficult motion. To do it effectively the children should be strong enough to hold tightly onto the parachute and be able to carefully listen to directions. The snap is mainly a wrist action. Hanging on firmly, flick both wrists in unison with a quick up-down motion, then stop. As they flick their wrists, they should also pull back slightly on the chute. This snapping motion takes practice. When it is done effectively the chute jumps.

15

 **FIRST SESSION**

Objectives: 1. To introduce the children to the parachute.
2. To introduce the thumbs-up grip.
3. To introduce the wave.
4. To learn the stop direction.

Additional Equipment: None

Body Position: Sitting

Hand Grips: Thumbs-up (two hands)

Begin

Each time you enjoy parachute play with the children, begin with the parachute in a bunched up position. Before the children come to the area where you'll be doing your parachute activities, bunch the parachute up, being sure that the edges of the chute are clearly visible, so that the children can easily grip the edge of the chute when it's time to begin.

As the children arrive in the area have them sit around the bunched up parachute. By always beginning in this manner, the children are immediately in a position where you can talk with them about the activities they will be doing, demonstrate holds, movements, and other simple directions, as well as let the children become involved with activities in a very low key manner. When the parachute is bunched up, there is less opportunity to move the chute before you've given them directions.

Introduce the Thumbs-Up Grip   While the children are sitting around the bunched up chute, introduce the first basic grip. Have them hold up their hands. Do several fingerplays to loosen up their hands and fingers.

10 LITTLE FINGERS

I have ten little fingers
They all belong to me.
I can make them do things
Do you want to see?
I can close them up tight.
I can open them wide.
I can hold them up high.
I can hold them down low
I can wave them to and fro,
And I can hold them just so.

FINGERS

These are my ten fingers.
They do whatever I say.
They help me when I'm eating.
They help me when I play.

Sometimes they work together.
Sometimes they work apart.
You can do so many things with them.
Can you think of one to start?

Dick Wilmes

(Let the children name what they do
with their fingers.)

After you've enjoyed several fingerplays have the children once again hold up both of their hands. While their hands are in the air (not holding the chute) have the children make fists with their fingers and palms and turn them so they face the ceiling. At the same time, have them point their thumbs to the ceiling. This is the Thumbs-Up grip.

While still sitting around the bunched up chute have the children hold the parachute with the Thumbs-Up grip. Tell them to grab a handful of the parachute material so that their fingers will be hiding under the chute and their thumbs will be peeking over the chute. When they are all holding the chute, have them look at another child and wiggle their thumbs at the person. Pick another child and wiggle at him.

Put the chute down and have the children shake their hands and wiggle their fingers. After the short rest, grab the chute again, use the Thumbs-Up grip and enjoy the first verse of *"Where is Thumpkin."* When you sing *"Run Away"* have the children lay their thumbs down on the top of the chute. Thus they have the Thumbs-Up grip they will use in many more activities.

**Introduce
the Wave**

Now that the children are familiar with one type of grip, have them quietly stand and hold the chute Thumbs-Up. While holding the chute, walk backwards until it is fully open. Sit down and lay the chute on the ground. Explain the wave as a motion in which each person moves both arms up and then both arms down. The group does not have to move in unison. Each person moves his arms as an individual. Do it first without the chute. Have the children say *"Up, down"* to themselves as they move their arms. This up and down rhythm will cause the parachute to form a shallow wave-like motion.

Now grab the chute Thumbs-Up. Enjoy doing the wave slowly. If you feel the children understand the motion do it a little faster and then very fast. Return to calm by waving the parachute slower, slower, slower. Rest.

Stop

Several times while the children are enjoying the wave, firmly say *"STOP."* When you do, the children should immediately quit. To enjoy the parachute activities, they will need to follow the *"STOP"* direction when it is given. It is best to introduce it as an important part of the first parachute experience and use it every time thereafter.

The children can repeat the wave from a standing position. Remember to use the Thumbs-Up grip and give the *"STOP"* direction often. Begin and end the movement slowly as you did from the sitting position.

19

Play 'Freeze'   Using the Thumbs-Up grip and the wave motion, enjoy playing Freeze. Put a musical record on the record player. As the music plays, the children dance and wave the chute. When you stop the music, the children should stop dancing and waving the parachute. Begin the record again and continue playing Freeze. When the record is over, change to one of a different tempo and play again. This activity is an excellent way to reinforce the *"STOP"* direction.

End   After you have played Freeze several times, the children will probably be tired. At this point, have them hold the parachute using the Thumbs-Up grip. Enjoy several slow waves to quiet down. Say *"STOP."* Then have them slowly walk the chute back to its bunched up shape and sit down around it. Talk a little about this first parachute experience.

SECOND SESSION

Objectives:
1. To review the thumbs-up grip.
2. To review the wave.
3. To introduce the thumbs-down grip.
4. To begin movements with the parachute.

Additional Equipment: None

Body Position: Sitting, Standing

Hand Grips: Thumbs-up and thumbs-down (two hands)

Begin

Start your activities by bunching up the parachute in the middle of your empty area. The children should sit around it in the beginning. At first have them grab the parachute with both hands using the Thumbs-Up grip as they have previously done. Look at each child's grip. Remind all of the children that their thumbs should be peeking over the parachute and their fingers hiding under it. While they are holding the chute with this grip, have them say *"Good Morning"* or *"Good Afternoon"* to their friends by wiggling their thumbs at each other and saying *"Hi."*

Introduce the Thumbs-Down Grip

Now introduce the second grip. The Thumbs-Down grip is the opposite of Thumbs-Up. In this position the children put their four fingers over the chute and their thumbs under the chute. Do it in the air first and then grab the parachute. While gripping the parachute in this manner, have them wiggle their fingers at a friend across the parachute. Now put the chute down and rest.

Moving

Until now the children have done activities from a fairly stationary position either sitting or standing. Now you're going to introduce movement while gripping the parachute. Begin with walking. Have the children grab the chute with the Thumbs-Down grip and begin walking clockwise in a circle. As you walk, chant *"Walk, Walk, Walk"* to the rhythm of your stride. When you decide you want to change the speed say *"STOP."* Then begin the walk chant at a different pace, maybe a little faster. As you walk to this quicker rhythm, remember to chant *"Walk, Walk, Walk"* as you go.

Not only can you vary the speeds with which you move, you can also change the movements. Once the children have learned to easily walk at different speeds, try sliding, galloping, or running. Use the *"STOP"* command between movements. Remember you can do any of these movements at different speeds. You can also use a Thumbs-Up or Thumbs-Down grip. No matter what movement, grip, or speed you use, always chant. This chant helps keep everyone moving at the same pace, assists with control, and definitely makes the activity more fun because the children's whole bodies are involved.

The last movement should be tiptoeing. By ending with a slow movement, the activity itself will quiet the children. Chant *"Tiptoe, Tiptoe, Tiptoe, Tiptoe"* in a quiet, almost whisper voice. You will feel the children relaxing as you move.

End

As they are finished tiptoeing, say *"STOP."* Now have them tiptoe the parachute slowly towards the middle to return it to its bunched up position. Sit around the chute and enjoy talking about what movements you just did. After the short discussion, tiptoe to the next activity of the day.

 # THIRD SESSION

Objectives:
1. To review the two basic grips.
2. To review the wave at different speeds.
3. To introduce kneeling with the parachute.
4. To introduce three parachute positions.
5. To use a ball with the parachute.

Additional Equipment: Beachball

Body Position: Kneeling, Standing

Hand Grips: Thumbs-up and thumbs-down (two hands)

Begin

The children will begin by sitting around the bunched up chute. Have them pretend that they are holding a parachute with a Thumbs-Up grip. (Quickly scan the group to be sure everyone's thumbs are up and their fists are closed and facing the ceiling.) With this grip have them pretend to wave the parachute slowly, a little faster, and now very fast. Switch to a Thumbs-Down grip and pretend to be waving the chute again.

The Kneeling Position

The children have enjoyed parachute activities from both a sitting and standing position. Kneeling is a third body position. In this position, the children will have more fun with the parachute movements than from the sitting position.

Have the children kneel around the bunched up chute. While kneeling have them grab the parachute with the Thumbs-Up grip. Now switch to Thumbs-Down. It takes time to make the switch so be sure to give the children a sufficient pause to reverse their hands. Do the switching several times. After the last switch, have the children lay the parachute on the ground and stand up.

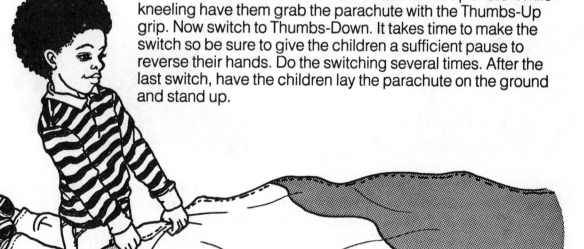

Three Parachute Positions

While standing around the bunched up chute, introduce the three basic parachute positions—down low by the knees, in the middle by the waist, and way up high in the sky. Have them pretend to grab the parachute with a Thumbs-Up grip. Now have them pretend to move it one time into each of the three positions. After this, play Simon Says (but no tricking), again pretending to hold the parachute.

Simon says, *"Thumbs-Up, kneel down and hold the parachute in the sky. STOP."*

Simon says, *"Thumbs-Up, sit down, parachute at your waist. STOP."*

Simon says, *"Thumbs-Down, stand up, parachute at your knees. STOP."*

Simon says, *"Listen carefully. Grab the chute, Thumbs-Up, stand, parachute at your waist and walk backwards to spread the parachute fully out."*

Play 'Simon Says'

While standing with the chute fully spread, continue playing Simon Says, only this time with the parachute in hand. (Give the commands at an appropriate pace for your group. As you do, walk around the chute helping any child who needs assistance.) After you've given 6-7 commands, transition to the next activity by commanding, Simon says, *"Thumbs-Up, kneel down, and parachute at your waist."*

Introduce the Beachball

While you're introducing the beachball, have the children sit back on their legs and relax their arms, but continue to hold the parachute with the Thumbs-Up grip. This is a fairly relaxing position and will give the children an opportunity to rest their arms.

Hold up the beachball. Tell the children that you are going to toss the ball onto the parachute. When you do they are going to use the slow wave motion and gently roll the ball around the parachute trying to keep it on the chute. If the ball rolls off (and it probably will) a child should retrieve it and toss it back onto the chute.

24

Play 'Around and Around— Back & Forth'

To begin playing, say *"Thumbs-Up, kneel straight, and hold the parachute at your waist."* When everyone is ready, toss the ball onto the parachute and let the children begin to slowly roll it around. Periodically say *"STOP"* and then let the children continue to roll the ball using a slow waving motion.

Play 'Simon Says'

After they have become comfortable with having an object on the parachute, say *"STOP"* and take the ball off. Vary the game in this manner. Use the Thumbs-Down grip, continue to kneel, but now you will give specific directions as to whom to roll the beachball to. Do this by again playing Simon Says. Get ready. Put the ball in front of a child.

Simon says, *"Angela, roll the ball to Paul."*

Simon says, *"Paul, roll the ball to Inez."*

Continue.

When rolling the ball from one person to another, the children around the person with ball will all gently wave the chute up in the direction of the other child. As the ball rolls across the chute towards the designated child, others will need to cooperate, directing the ball toward the right child by using the slow waving motion.

End

Conclude your parachute play by using three more commands:

Simon says, *"Eric, roll the ball to Mrs. Wilmes."*

Simon says, *"Stand up, slowly walk the parachute to the middle, and bunch it up on the floor."*

When the children are in the middle

Simon says, *"Tiptoe to lunch"* (or whatever the next activity will be.)

 # FOURTH SESSION

Objectives: 1. To use the wave in the three different parachute positions.
2. To introduce the jerk motion.
3. To introduce holding the parachute with one hand.

Additional Equipment: Washable marker, beachball

Body Position: Standing

Hand Grips: Thumbs-up and thumbs-down (two hands-one hand)

Begin   While the children are sitting around the bunched up chute, enjoy several fingerplays to loosen up their hands and fingers.

BUSY FINGERS

This is the way my fingers stand,
Fingers stand, fingers stand,
This is the way my fingers stand,
So early in the morning.

This is the way they dance about,
Dance about, dance about,
This is the way they dance about,
So early in the morning.

This is the way I fold my hands,
Fold my hands, fold my hands,
This is the way I fold my hands,
So early in the morning.

This is the way they go to rest,
Go to rest, go to rest,
This is the way they go to rest,
So early in the morning.

COUNTING

One, two, three, four
I can even count some more.
Five, six, seven, eight
All my fingers stand up straight.
Nine, ten are my thumb men.

After the fingerplays, have the children stand, turn their backs to the parachute and grab the parachute with a Thumbs-Up grip. Walk forward with the parachute until it is fully spread out. Then turn around, use a Thumbs-Up grip and hold the parachute at their knees. To check everyone's grip have them wiggle their thumbs at each other.

Waving

While in this position, they should begin waving the chute slowly. As they wave it, have them sing *"Row, Row, Row Your Boat"* to the rhythm of their wave.

Have them move the parachute to their waists. Toss a beachball onto the parachute. Pretend that the ball is a boat and that a storm is coming up and the boat is being tossed around in the water. Wave the parachute a little faster. The storm continues to build up and the boat is really being rocked around. Wave very fast. All storms eventually subside and so does this one. Soon the boat is gently rocking once again. Wave the parachute slowly. Sing *"Row, Row, Row Your Boat"* slowly and quietly.

Rest. While doing so, talk about waving the parachute at different speeds. How do their arms feel? What speed was the most fun? Why?

After your discussion, have the children grab the parachute Thumbs-Up, hold it above their heads, and wave it slowly for a short time. While they are waving the chute, have them look at their friends under the chute. Lower the chute and rest. Holding the chute in the sky is very tiring so only do it for a short time.

**Introduce
the Jerk**

As opposed to the wave which is an up and down motion of the parachute, the jerk is a side-to-side motion. Have the children grab the parachute Thumbs-Down. Quickly go around the group and mark an X on everyone's right hand and an O on their left hand. (If all of the children can differentiate their left and right hands this is unnecessary.)

Holding tightly to the chute, have everyone jerk the chute in the direction of their X hand (right), now to their O hand (left), back to the right and then to the left. Stop. When the group understands the motion, jerk the chute at different speeds. The children should chant the word "*jerk*" as they do it. Range from a very slow movement to a rapid one.

Toss a beachball onto the chute. Wave the chute and then discuss what happened to the ball. Keeping the ball on the chute, do the jerk motion at various speeds. What happened to the beachball when the parachute moved side-to-side? Did the ball bounce the same when the parachute was waved and jerked?

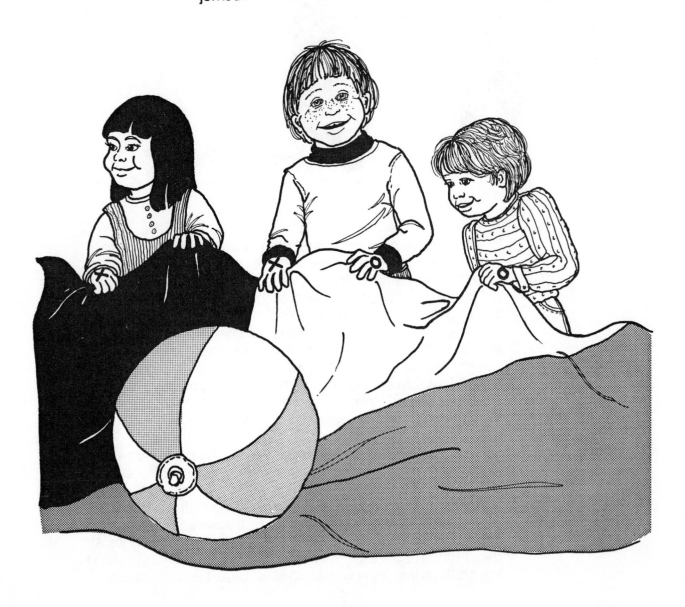

Introduce Holding the Parachute With One Hand

During a previous parachute session, the children held the parachute with two hands and did simple movements as they rotated in the same direction and in a circle. From the standing position and Thumbs-Down have them hold the parachute waist high and enjoy several of the movements again—walk, gallop, run and then a slow tiptoe. They should remember to chant as they move. Say *"STOP"* between movements and before a change of speed.

Now that their minds and bodies have been refreshed, have the children stop. Tell them that they are going to continue doing movements, but now they are going to grip the parachute with only one hand. Have them all face in the same direction and grab the parachute using the Thumbs-Down grip.

Begin walking at an average pace holding the parachute waist high. After a little while say *"STOP."* Switch hands, use the Thumbs-Up grip and begin walking again. They should remember to hold on tightly.

Continue enjoying different simple movements. Remember to switch directions for variety. Give the children enough time to make all of the adjustments before they begin each new movement.

End

After the last movement, have them once again grab the parachute with both hands. Lift the parachute to the sky and begin to slowly walk to the middle. About halfway there, have them lower the parachute to their waist and walk the rest of the way. Lay the parachute down and sit around it. As the teacher calls each child's name, the child should tell the rest of the children where he's going next and then he may leave the parachute area and continue with the next activity.

29

FIFTH SESSION

Objectives: 1. To review all of the parachute grips, speeds, positions and movements.
2. To introduce the wave in unison.

Additional Equipment: None

Body Position: Standing, Sitting

Hand Grips: Thumbs-up, thumbs-down (one hand-two hands)

Begin

Sit around the parachute. When everyone is ready, simply have the children shake their hands and wiggle their fingers. Say *"STOP."* Then give them specific directions, such as *"Wiggle your fingers way up high"* or *"Shake your hands near your knees"* or *"Make the Thumbs-Up grip and wiggle your thumbs."* The last direction should be *"Grab the parachute with the Thumbs-Up grip, stand, hold it above your head, and walk backwards until it is fully spread out."* When it is completely out have them lower the chute to their waist.

Play 'Follow the Leader'

The children have learned many ways to manipulate the parachute in a short period of time.

- Two ways to grip it.
- How to wave it.
- How to jerk it.
- How to wave and jerk it at different speeds.
- How to move with it using either a one hand or a two hand grip.
- How to enjoy activities from a sitting, standing and kneeling position.
- How to hold the parachute in three basic places—at their knees, waist, and over their head.

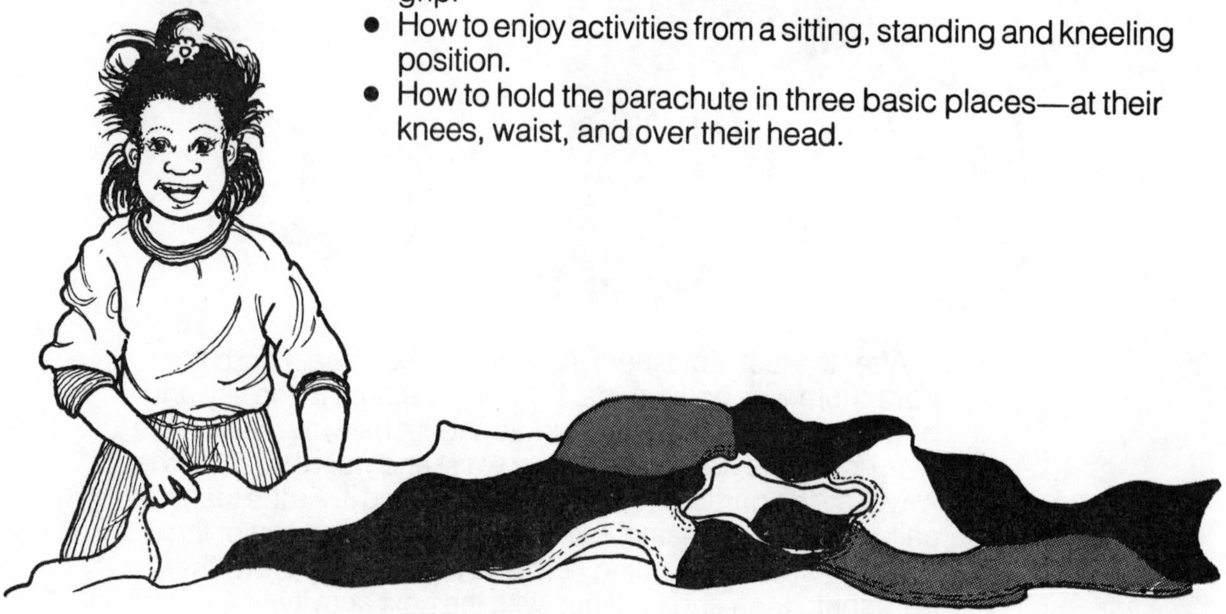

Using different combinations of skills the children know, play Follow the Leader. The teacher should be the leader. The children should watch what grip is used, where the parachute is being held, what body position the teacher chooses, and then the specific movement. Do the movement for a while, say *"STOP"* and then create a new combination. Enjoy seven or eight combinations with the children. Remember to go at a pace that is comfortable for the children.

After they have enjoyed Follow the Leader, have the children sit around the spread out parachute.

Introduce the Wave in Unison

Until now the children have been using a both arms up and both arms down waving motion, as individuals, to create shallow waves. When they rolled the beachball around and back and forth, they were aware of working together with several other children. Now, however, the group will take a big step in parachute play. They will begin to all move their arms together. All of the children will go up together and then down together—thus creating a giant wave.

While in the sitting position have them grab the parachute using the Thumbs-Up grip. Tell them they are going to move the parachute together. When you say *"Up"* they will lift the parachute about chest high. When you say *"Down"* they will lower it. Do this *"Up together—Down together"* motion several times. Talk about what happens to the parachute when they all move in unison.

31

To create an even more dramatic effect of this motion, have the children wave in unison from a standing position. First they should move in several steps so the chute has some slack in it. Then they can begin to wave. In the beginning, be careful not to let the parachute get too high, for the children may not be strong enough to control it. After awhile they'll all feel comfortable as the parachute forms giant waves over their heads. To get the chute even higher, create additional slack by having the children take several more steps towards the middle.

End

Before you wave for the last time, tell the children that the next time they wave the parachute over their heads, you will give the verbal signal *"Let go."* They should watch it float to the ground. When it is on the ground, have them grab it, walk it to the middle and sit down.

This has been an exciting and strenuous day with the parachute. Before they leave, play a quiet record. As it is playing, have the children slowly wave the bunched up chute. Then whisper *"John, go to art. Sarah, your turn to play with the blocks"* and so on until all of the children have left the parachute and are involved in other activities.

SIXTH SESSION

Objectives: 1. To review the wave.
2. To review the jerk.
3. To introduce the flip-flop.

Additional Equipment: Beachball, marker

Body Position: Standing

Hand Grips: Thumbs-up and thumbs-down (two hands)

Begin

The children sit around the bunched up parachute. Walk around and put an X on their right hand and an O on their left hand. Have them grab the parachute using both hands with a Thumbs-Up grip. Then give rapid-fire commands changing the grips.

> *"Two hands, Thumbs-Down"*
> *"O (left) hand only, Thumbs-Down"*
> *"X (right) hand only, Thumbs-Up"*
> *"Two hands, Thumbs-Up"*
> *"O (left) hand only, Thumbs-Up"*
> *·"X (right) hand only, Thumbs-Down"*

Introduce the Flip-Flop

After they have finished the short warm-up exercise, have them put the parachute down. Until now they have moved the parachute by using a side-to-side jerking motion or a both arms up and both arms down motion. When they have done this individually, they have created a shallow waving movement. When they have gone up and down in unison, they have created giant waves.

Now they are going to alternate arms—one arm up and one arm down. Have them grab the parachute with a Thumbs-Up grip. Start by having them slightly lift up their X (right) hand. Now bring the X (right) hand down and lift the O (left) hand. Continue this alternating motion at a slow speed until you think they have the rhythm of this new motion called flip-flop.

Now stand up, continue grabbing the parachute with the Thumbs-Up grip. Walk the parachute until it is fully spread out. As the children are walking it out, have them slowly flip-flop the parachute.

Now that it is fully spread out, slowly flip-flop the parachute. This will be slightly more tiring than when it was bunched up because you have the entire weight of the chute. Now let the children flip-flop a little faster, a little faster, and then very fast. Bring them back to calm by reversing the order, a little slower, slower still, very slow. Remember to let your voice become quieter as the parachute slows down.

33

While resting, enjoy a fingerplay to get the wiggles out.

MY WIGGLES

I wiggle my fingers,
I wiggle my toes.
I wiggle my shoulders,
I wiggle my nose.
Now the wiggles are out of me,
And I'm just as still as I can be.

Using the Thumbs-Down grip have them pick the chute up again. Say *"Mary, wiggle your fingers at Angela."* Continue giving children the opportunity to wiggle their fingers at each other.

During the first session you enjoyed the first verse of *"Where is Thumpkin."* Now enjoy the rest of the rhyme. Begin with the Thumbs-Up grip and sing the first verse. This time when you sing *"Run Away, Run Away"* have the children switch to the Thumbs-Down grip. Now continue the rhyme. Each time one of the fingers *'runs away'* have the children lay the appropriate finger on top of the chute. When you're finished, all of the fingers will be gripping the chute from above and the thumbs will be underneath. Thus you have a Thumbs-Down grip.

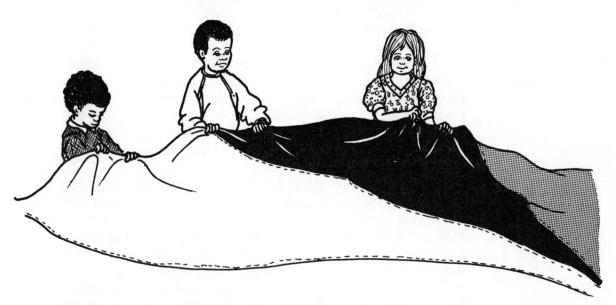

Waving

Have the children grab the parachute using the Thumbs-Down grip, stand up and slowly walk backwards until the parachute is fully spread out. Enjoy several waves at different speeds from a standing position. Be sure to use the word *"STOP"* before you switch to another speed. Thus you might say *"STOP. OK, let's wave a little faster."* Do that for awhile and say *"STOP. This time let's go real fast."* When tired, say *"STOP. Wave very slowly."* Now they are ready to listen to instructions and then enjoy the next activity.

**Play
'Beachball
Bounce'**

In this game the children really need to listen to your commands. The first time the children play this game have them use the Thumbs-Up grip and keep the parachute around their waists. On other days, however, have them try the movements at their knees or over their head.

Toss the beachball onto the chute. First have the children wave the parachute slowly. What is happening to the ball? Continue the game by giving different directions, changing the motion and speed of the parachute.

"Flip-flop very slowly.   STOP."
"Wave very fast.   STOP."
"Jerk at a medium speed.   STOP."
"Wave in unison slowly.   STOP."
"Roll the ball around the parachute.   STOP."
And so on . . .

End

The last command should be *"Flip-flop slowly and walk the parachute back to the middle."* Take the beachball off the chute. Have the children sit down. Talk about the three different motions. Which one is most tiring? Do they like to move the chute quickly or slowly? If they wanted the beachball to go very fast, what motion and speed would they use? Which motion is most relaxing? Did the beachball ever fly off the parachute? What motion were they using?

After the discussion, have the children grab the bunched up parachute with either the Thumbs-Up or Thumbs-Down grip, either one hand or two. Now go around the parachute, letting each child say what he is going to do next. After he has decided on his next activity, he should wiggle his thumbs or fingers and say *"Good-bye"* as he transitions to his next activity.

# SEVENTH SESSION

Objectives: 1. To review the different parachute positions.
2. To learn more movements.
3. To introduce the snap.

Additional Equipment: 15-20 cotton balls, popcorn popper, popcorn kernels, bowl, salt

Body Position: Standing

Hand Grips: Thumbs-up (two hands)

Begin

Have the children stand around the bunched up parachute. Enjoy chanting the rhyme *"Head, Shoulders, Knees, and Toes."*

HEAD, SHOULDERS, KNEES, AND TOES
Head, shoulders, knees, and toes,
Knees and toes, knees and toes,
Head, shoulders, knees and toes,
Eyes, ears, mouth and nose.

Ask the children if they can remember the three places where they have held the parachute—knees, waist, and over their head. Standing around the chute have them grab it Thumbs-Down and move it from their knees, to their waist, to over their head, and back down to their waist and then their knees. When it is at their knees, have them walk it out.

Moving

Almost any simple movement that one can do without a parachute can also be done with it. In previous sessions, the children have enjoyed walking, sliding, galloping, running, and tiptoeing. Begin with these movements, using either one or two hands, everyone using either the Thumbs-Up or Thumbs-Down grip. Once again remember to chant the movement at the rhythm the children are moving and to say *"STOP"* between movements.

Once they are warmed up, begin introducing new movements, hopping, bouncing up and down in place, skipping, shuffling, marching, and weaving. For added variation have the children periodically reverse directions.

If the record *We All Live Together* Volume II by Scelesa and Millang is available, enjoy moving to the song 'Listen and Move.' It is great fun after the children are comfortable with movement and can stop, change, and start movements easily. (Everyone will need to listen carefully for the changing movements.) The rhythm of the music will dictate the speed at which they are to move.

Introduce the Snap

Have everyone sit around the parachute and hold it with two hands using the Thumbs-Down grip. As with the waving motion, the snapping motion is both up - both down. Unlike the two motions, waving and flip-flop, use only your wrists to make the parachute move, thus it is both wrists up - both wrists down. As you move your wrists, you also slightly pull back on the chute.

When you say *"Snap"* have everyone quickly click their wrists one time. Say *"STOP."* Repeat the motion several times in a row — *"Snap, STOP, Snap, STOP, Snap, STOP, Snap, STOP."*

Play 'Popping Corn'

Have the children sit around the parachute. Talk about the entire process of making popcorn. Begin by gathering all of the ingredients, pouring in a little oil, and adding the kernels. What happens to the kernels as they cook? First you hear one or two go pop. Then several more and all of a sudden you hear all of them exploding in the popper. At this point teach the children the *Popcorn Song,* sung to the tune of *"Row, Row, Row Your Boat."*

POPCORN SONG

Pop, pop, pop your corn,
Pop it big and white.

Popping, popping, popping, popping
Popping 'til it's white.

37

As if on cue, the popping begins to subside. Soon you only hear one or two kernels. Finally, silence. Open the popper and the delicious white snack is almost ready. What is next? Of course, pour it in a bowl and add a little salt.

After discussing the popcorn making process, have the children pick up the parachute Thumbs-Down. Toss one cotton ball onto the parachute. Say *"We're going to pretend that the cotton balls are the popcorn. First we hear only one or two kernels popping."* Using the snapping motion, begin to pop the popcorn. Gradually add all of the balls. Change to a rapid flip-flop motion while all of the kernels are popping. Return to the snapping motion as the popping subsides. Sing the *Popcorn Song* several times as the corn pops.

End

If the cotton balls have not flown off of the chute, take them off. Have the children walk the parachute back to its bunched up position.

Now everyone move to the snack area to make some real popcorn. While waiting for the popcorn to begin popping, enjoy these two popcorn rhymes:

EZ POPPER

Take a little oil.
Take a little seed.
Put them in a popper,
And heat is all you need.
    Dick Wilmes

THE POPCORN KERNEL

I am a popcorn kernel,
On the electric range,
With oil to my ankles,
Waiting for the change.

Pop, pop it's started happening,
The noise has just begun.
Pop, pop, there it goes again.
It sounds like lots of fun.

Explosions to the left of me.
Explosions to the right.
I'm just about to blow my top,
I really think I might.
BANG!!!
    Dick Wilmes

 # EIGHTH SESSION

Objectives: 1. To review the four parachute motions.
2. To introduce going under the parachute.

Additional Equipment: Beachball

Body Position: Standing

Hand Grips: Thumbs-down (two hands)

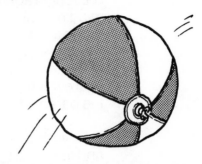

Begin

The children should sit around the bunched up parachute. Tell them that today they are going to play several games under the parachute. Until now, they have done all of the activities grabbing onto the edge of the chute, moving in a variety of ways, and/or controlling a ball on top of the parachute.

Going under the chute is very exciting, but for some people also a little frightening, so as the children play, be very aware of feelings. It can also be very tiring, for as one or more children are under the chute, the others are usually holding it above their heads. Remember to provide enough resting opportunities.

While sitting, simply have the children grab the parachute Thumbs-Down, lift it above their heads, and duck under it. Now come out and lower the chute. What was it like under the chute? Now have them lift it again and duck under. This time turn to one of the people sitting next to them and say *"Hi."*

Using the Thumbs-Down grip, have them stand and walk the parachute out.

Play 'Beachball Bounce'

When it is fully spread, toss the beachball onto the center of the parachute. Always using the Thumbs-Down grip, vary the motion, the speed, and the parachute position when giving commands:

- *Waist high, wave the parachute slowly. Stop.*
- *Over your head, snap the parachute quickly one time. STOP.*
- *Waist high, wave the chute in unison until it looms overhead. STOP. What happened to the ball?*
- *At your knees, flip-flop very fast. STOP.*

Continue and then end with a relaxing slow command.

**Play
'Shaking Hands'**

Now the children are ready to enjoy several under-the-chute activities. (Remember the two cautions explained above.) In the first activity, have the group hold the parachute above their heads. You call out two children's names. They run under the chute to the center, shake hands and then run back to their places. Lower the chute. Ask the group, *"Who shook hands under the chute?"* After they answer, have them raise the parachute again; you call out two more names. They run to the middle, shake hands and back again. Lower the chute. Ask the group to name the four children who have shaken hands under the chute. Repeat the activity and then ask who are the six children who have shaken hands under the chute. Continue until everyone has had the opportunity to shake hands under the parachute.

Moving

Have the children hold up the parachute. Call a child's name and tell him a movement. He must do that movement around the inner edge of the chute. He stops back at his place. Rest between each child.

- Run
- Slide
- Gallop
- March
- Walk quickly

- Hop
- Skip
- Tiptoe
- Crawl
- Leap

Play 'Sammy Is Wearing'

In this game have the children sit down, hold the parachute way above their heads, look at another child and remember the color of one piece of clothing that the child is wearing. Now lower the chute. Call on a child. That child should say *"Sammy (or whoever the child is he was looking at) is wearing something red."* Sammy stands up and the group calls out what piece of clothing is red. Then Sammy says *"Carla is wearing something brown."* Carla stands up and the group calls out what Carla is wearing that is brown. Carla continues.

When half of the children have had a turn, have the group grab the chute again, lift it high over their heads, find a different child and remember the color of one piece of clothing that the child is wearing. Lower the chute and continue as before.

End

Have the children walk the chute to the middle. When they are there, have them remain standing. Play Peek-a-Boo several times. Have everyone put their head under the chute. When you say *"Now,"* they should quickly uncover their heads and say *"Peek-a-Boo"* to a person standing near them.

After a while, have them lay the chute down and tiptoe to their next activity.

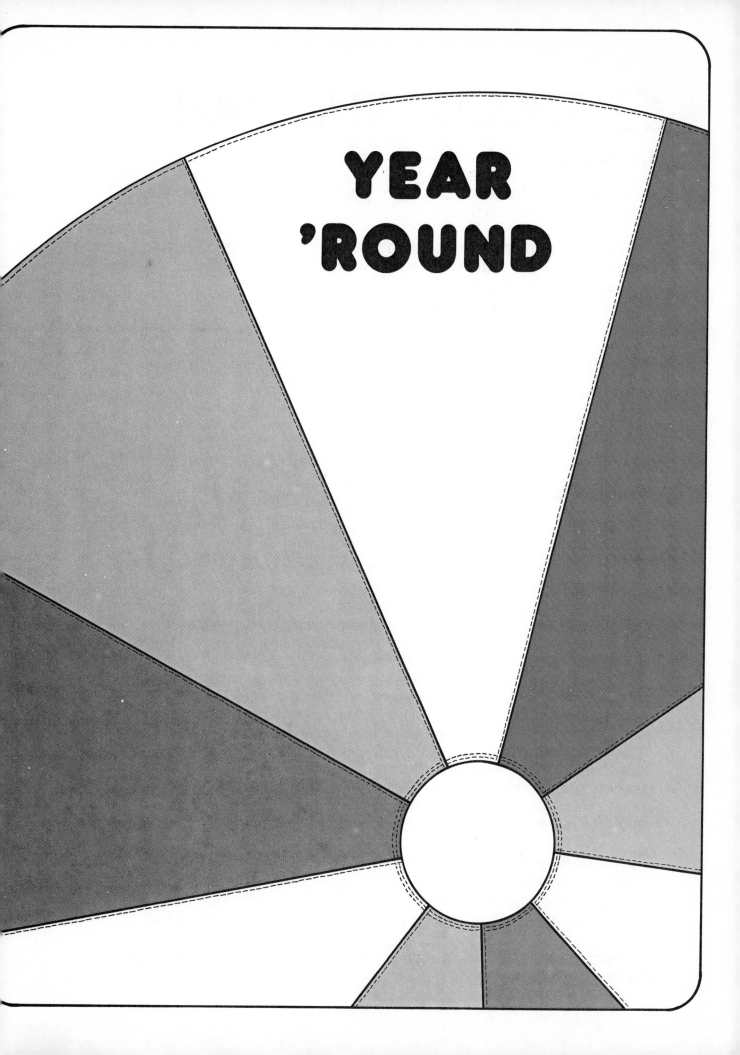

YEAR 'ROUND

# AROUND THE CHUTE

Suggested Units: Letters, Self-Concept

Additional Equipment: Large name cards (Write each child's name on a large piece of posterboard.)

Warm-Up Exercise: Standing, grab the bunched up parachute using the Thumbs-Up grip. Do a series of exercises while holding the parachute.
- *"Touch your toes three times."*
- *"Stretch your arms up high, then way down low."*
- *"Bend forward."*
- *"Run in place."*
- *"Sit down."* (Explain the main activity and teach the rhyme.)
- *"Stand up and stretch the chute out, running backwards."*

Main Activity

Body Position: Standing

Hand Grip: Thumbs-Up (two hands)

Parachute Position: Waist

Parachute Motion: Taut

Directions: First teach the children this rhyme.

"Eric, Eric, (name will change each time) what do you say!
Run (movement will change each time) around the chute today."

   After the children know the rhyme, have them stand and grab the parachute with the Thumbs-Up grip. Together they chant the rhyme, letting the teacher call out the child's name, what movement he will be doing, and then allowing him to move around the chute. Continue in this manner.

   Do this activity another day using a slight variation. Instead of the teacher calling out each child's name, this time s/he should hold up a namecard. The child whose name is on the card should let go of the parachute. Now everyone knows who's going to move. The children chant the first line of the rhyme using the child's name. When the chant gets to the second line, everyone is quiet and the designated child tells what movement he would like to do around the parachute. He says *" Hop around the chute today."* Then he begins to hop. The children can encourage the moving child by quietly chanting *"Hop, hop, hop, hop."* Continue, letting other children move around the chute.

Concluding Activity: Using the familiar chant, the teacher says,

"Children, children what do you say!
Time to bunch up the chute today."

   Then have them walk the chute to the middle.

Extension: As an art activity, have the children collage scraps of colored paper over the letters in their names.

UP AND DOWN

Suggested Units: Opposites

Additional Equipment: None

Warm-Up Exercise: As the children come to the bunched up chute, have them stand and grab it Thumbs-Down. Walk the chute out backwards. When fully out begin singing a variation of *"Here We Go 'Round the Mulberry Bush."* The children should move as directed by the song.

Here we jog 'round the Mulberry Bush
The Mulberry Bush, the Mulberry Bush
Here we jog 'round the Mulberry Bush
So early Monday morning.

Repeat the song, changing the movements to run, walk, slide, hop, gallop. The last one should be sit. Then explain the main activity.

Main Activity

Body Position: Standing

Hand Grip: Thumbs-Down

Parachute Position: Waist, over their heads

Parachute Motion: Wave, flip-flop, snap, taut

Directions: Have the children stand and hold the chute using the Thumbs-Down grip. Reinforce opposite words through a variety of movements:

UP - DOWN   Slowly raise the chute in an upward motion. As they do, have them chant *"Up, up, up, up."* Then lower it. As they do that, chant *"Down, down, down, down."* Another time talk about how the chute is getting *"higher, higher, higher, higher"* as it is being raised and *"lower, lower, lower, lower"* as it comes down.

FAST - SLOW   Have the children stand and hold the chute taut. They should slowly pass the chute to the right. As they do, they should chant, *"Slowly, slowly, slowly, slowly."* Reverse the direction and pass it quickly. As they do, chant *"Fast, fast, fast, fast."*

LOUD - QUIET   Have the children flip-flop the chute fast enough so it creates a noise. Now have them snap the chute hard. At each snap have the children shout *"Loud."* Change to a slow, waving motion. Listen carefully. Do they hear a noise? As they wave they should whisper *"Quiet, quiet, quiet, quiet."*

IN - OUT   Have the children stand and hold the chute taut. The children should begin chanting *"In, in, in, in."* As they chant they should walk towards the center of the circle. Now walk back. As they do, chant *"Out, out, out, out."*

UNDER - OVER   Have the children stand and hold the chute with one hand. When the teacher says *"Put your hand under the chute"* the children should put their free hand under the chute. When the teacher says *"Put your hand over the chute"* have the children stick their free hand on the top of the chute. Continue using other body parts such as elbow, head, or thumb.

Concluding Activity: Bunch up the chute by walking backwards to the center.

Extension: All day long have the children walk backwards through all doorways.

GOING TO THE ZOO

Suggested Units: Zoo, Animals

Additional Equipment: None

Warm-Up Exercise: When all of the children are standing around the bunched up chute, have them grab it using a Thumbs-Down grip. Have them think of an exercise that the group can do while holding onto the chute. Quickly go around the chute and have each child whisper his exercise to you. Walk the chute out. Have the children hold the chute above their heads. One child goes under the chute, demonstrates his exercise, such as jumping up and down four times and runs back out. Lower the chute and everyone do the exercise. Raise the chute, another child demonstrates an exercise. Continue. The teacher demonstrates last. S/he goes under the chute and sits down. When s/he comes out, everyone sits around the chute. Explain the main activity.

Main Activity

Body Position: Standing

Hand Grip: Thumbs-Down (both hands)

Parachute Position: Over their head

Parachute Motion: Taut

Directions: Sit around the chute. Have the children close their eyes and pretend they are at the zoo. They should picture all of the different animals. After thinking for several minutes, have each child choose an animal. The teacher should walk quickly around the chute and have each child whisper his animal to him/her.

After everyone has an animal (there can be duplicates), have the children stand and lift the chute above their heads. Call on a child to go under the chute and pretend to be the animal he has chosen. As the children are holding up the chute, they try to guess what animal is being portrayed. When they guess, the child comes out and the chute is lowered to the ground. While the chute is on the ground, have the children standing next to each other pair off. Have them act like that animal to each other. After the antics, grip and raise the chute, have another child pretend to be an animal and then the group guesses what this next animal in the zoo is. Continue until everyone completes his trip to the zoo.

Concluding Activity: Have each child make the noise of his chosen animal as the group walks the chute back to its bunched up position. Does the classroom sound like a zoo?

Extension: Put plastic or wooden animals in the block area.

# POP-FLIES

Suggested Units: Summer, Balls

Additional Equipment: Beachball, several large sponge-type balls

Warm-Up Exercise: As the children gather around the bunched up chute, have them grab it with the Thumbs-Down grip and walk backwards until it is fully spread out. Once spread, have them wave the chute using different speeds. Then toss the beachball onto the chute. First have them use the waving motion to roll the ball back and forth across the chute. Next have them roll it around the edge of the chute.

Take the beachball off of the chute and toss the sponge-type ball onto it. As with the beachball, use the waving motion to direct the ball around the chute. After waving the chute, change to the snap motion. First snap the ball several times in a row, so it jumps up and down on the chute. Next, put the ball on one side of the chute. Snap it three or four times trying to get it to jump across the chute to the other side. Work together. After you've done this several times, have the children lay the chute on the floor and sit down. Explain the main activity.

Main Activity

Body Position: Kneeling

Hand Grip: Thumbs-Down (two hands)

Parachute Position: On the floor

Parachute Motion: Snap

Directions: Have all of the children take off their shoes and kneel evenly spaced around the edge of the chute. Pick two or three children to walk onto the middle of the chute and kneel down facing the children who are around the edge of the chute. The children kneeling around the edge, grab the chute, Thumbs-Down.

Give one of the children around the edge the sponge ball. Have him toss it to one of the children in the middle. That child catches it and tosses it back to someone else. Play catch for a little while. After they understand the back and forth procedure, have a child on the edge of the parachute put the ball on the chute. This time, all of the children around the ball lift the chute with a real hard snap. The ball will fly into the air. The children in the middle should try to catch the pop-fly. (You can also designate which child should catch the ball each time.) When a child gets it, he throws it to another child. The children immediately snap the chute and a child in the middle catches the ball again. Rotate the children in the middle so everyone has the opportunity to catch and to snap.

If the snapping motion is too difficult or you want to slow down the activity, let the children use the waving motion to roll the ball to the middle and children will catch ground-balls rather than pop-flies.

Concluding Activity: Have the children lay the chute on the ground, kneel around it, and grab the edge with both hands. Then slowly, very slowly, begin to roll the chute up. When the chute is all rolled up, have the children scoot back and form a circle. Sing the song, *"This Old Man"* and let the children enjoy rolling their arms around and around.

48

 # SCARF DANCING

Suggested Units: Summer, Air/Wind, Colors

Additional Equipment: 6-8 different colored nylon scarves; record with slow, quiet music

Warm-Up Exercise: As the children come to the bunched up parachute, tell them to remain standing and grab the chute using the Thumbs-Up grip. Have them walk the chute until it is fully spread out. As they walk, they should wave the chute gently.

When the chute is fully out, play 'Simon Says,' concentrating on directions which use the four varieties of parachute motions—wave, jerk, flip-flop, and snap.

SIMON SAYS, "Flip-flop the chute very fast."
SIMON SAYS, "Wave the chute in unison until it gets high over your head."
SIMON SAYS, "Snap the chute four times."
Continue with more directions.
SIMON SAYS, "Sit, lay the parachute on the ground." Explain the main activity.

Main Activity

Body Position: Standing

Hand Grip: Thumbs-Up

Parachute Position: Waist

Parachute Motion: Wave, jerk, flip-flop, snap

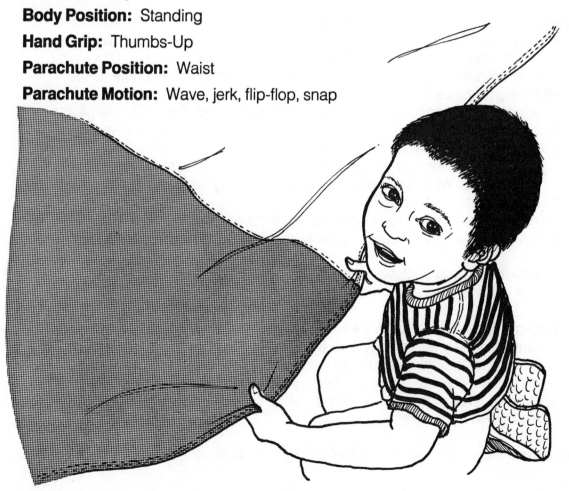

Directions: Hold up each scarf and have the group quietly call out its color. Give the scarf to a child and have him tuck it into his waist or drape it over his shoulder. After all of the scarves have been distributed, have the children stand and begin to wave the chute slowly. Call on a child to toss his *blue* scarf onto the chute. Is the scarf beginning to dance?

Change to a slow flip-flop, then a slow jerk, and last a snap. Stop. Did the blue scarf dance as the parachute moved? Which motion caused the scarf to move the most? The least? How high did the scarf leap up?

Change the speed of the four motions. Now what is happening to the scarf? Add several more scarves. What do the scarves look like as they are floating through the air? Which scarf goes the highest?

Accelerate to a very fast speed using the four motions. Add the rest of the scarves. Discuss what type of dancing the scarves do when the chute moves so quickly.

Play a slow, quiet record. Move the chute to the rhythm of the music. Enjoy watching the scarves dance.

Concluding Activity: Before walking the chute in, collect the dancing scarves. Start with the ones that are near the children. Say *"Misha, take the red scarf."* When the ones within easy reach have been gathered, wave the chute to move the other scarves within reach. When a scarf gets close to a child, have him get it. Continue until all of the scarves are off of the parachute.

Walk the chute to its bunched up position.

Extension: Take the scarves outside and run with them as if they were kites.

50

🪂 MOVE QUICKLY

Suggested Units: Numbers, Body Awareness

Additional Equipment: None

Warm-Up Exercise: Leaving the parachute bunched up, have the children stand and form a wide circle around the chute. Moving in a circle, do several large body movements, such as sliding, galloping, running, and crawling. Several times, call *"Stop"* and reverse directions. Have the last movement bring the children close to the parachute and then sit down.

   Explain the main activity. Before the children bring the chute out, have them think of a movement they will use when it is their turn to move quickly. Go around the circle and have each child tell the others what movement he's chosen. Now have the group stand, turn their backs to the parachute, grab it with the Thumbs-Down grip, and slide as they bring it out. When everyone is out, have them turn around, continuing to grab the chute with a Thumbs-Down grip.

Main Activity

Body Position: Standing

Hand Grip: Thumbs-Down (both hands)

Parachute Position: Over their heads

Parachute Motion: Taut

Directions: When the parachute is fully spread out, have the children raise it above their heads. Then call a child's name. That child should use his movement to quickly cross under the chute to a new place on the chute. After he has grabbed the chute in his new place, everyone can lower the chute to his waist. The child who did the movement says *"I skated under the chute."* Continuing to grab onto the chute the children skate around the circle chanting *"Skating, skating, skating"* as they move. Say *"Stop"* to finish.

   Continue in the same manner. Everyone lift the chute over his head. Say another child's name. He should do a movement under the chute to another place on the chute. When he's across, lower the chute, and have everyone do the movement. (If a child does a movement which cannot be done while grabbing the parachute, such as twirling or crawling, then simply lay the parachute down and crawl or twirl around it.)

   After much activity, gallop the chute back to the middle.

Concluding Activity: As each child leaves the area, have him use a different movement. *"Sam, gallop to snacks"* or *"Anita, crawl to the table."*

Extension: Enjoy playing 'Follow the Leader' both indoors and outdoors.

BOUNCE THE BALL

Suggested Units: Numbers

Additional Equipment: Large rubber ball

Warm-Up Exercise: Have the children stand around the bunched up parachute and grab it using the Thumbs-Down grip. When you call out a number, have the children snap the chute that number of times, counting as they snap. Repeat with five or six different numbers.

Explain the main activity. As each person walks the parachute out, have him count his steps. How many steps did each person take? Did everyone use the same number of steps?

Main Activity

Body Position: Standing

Hand Grip: Thumbs-Down (both hands)

Parachute Position: Over their heads

Parachute Motion: Taut

Directions: When the parachute is fully spread out, have the children hold the parachute taut over their heads. Give the ball to a child. Have him run under the chute, put the ball on the floor in the middle of the parachute area, and then run back to his space on the parachute. When he gets back, the children should lower the parachute to their waists. Now the activity is set up.

When you give the *"Up"* signal, all of the children raise the chute above their heads. Call out a child's name. Tell him to run to the middle and bounce the ball a certain number of times. He then runs under the chute, picks up the ball, and begins bouncing it. As he bounces, the group of children count. When finished, he puts the ball down and runs back to his place. When he gets back to his place, everyone lowers the parachute for a rest.

Continue to play by having the children raise the parachute up, calling on another child to bounce the ball while the group counts, and then having the child run back to his place. Remember to rest between each child or at least between every two children.

After everyone has had a turn, lift the chute up one more time, have a child run under it, pick up the ball, and give it to the teacher. While the chute is still over their heads, have the children begin walking the chute toward the middle. When the chute sags to the ground have them lower their arms and finish bunching up the chute.

Concluding Activity: Have each child count how many steps it takes him to get to his next activity. When everyone has left the parachute area, go around and ask each child how many steps he took to get to the book shelf, art corner, etc.

Extension: Have large rubber balls available for the children to use outside.

52

BUILD AN IGLOO

Suggested Units: Building, Families

Additional Equipment: None

Warm-Up Exercise: When the children gather around the parachute have them stand, grab it using the Thumbs-Down grip, and hold it at their waist. While around the bunched up chute, have them lower it to the ground while counting *"5, 4, 3, 2, 1"* pause and lift it to their waist *"1, 2, 3, 4, 5."* Do this several times. Walk the chute out.

Now that it is fully out, have the children remain standing and lower the chute to the ground. This time as the children raise the chute, have them breathe in; as they lower the chute, breathe out. The teacher should count as the children are raising and lowering the chute. Do this several times. Have them kneel and do it. Have them sit and do it.

While sitting, explain the main activity.

Main Activity

Body Position: Standing

Hand Grip: Thumbs-Down

Parachute Position: Knees, waist, above their heads

Parachute Motion: Long, slow waves done together

53

Directions: The children should use the Thumbs-Down grip and stand. With the parachute in a fully spread out position have the children take a short step forward to give a little slack in the parachute.

Then have them lower the chute to just below their knees. Slowly bring the chute up with a long, sweeping wave motion. Bring it down to about waist high. Raise it up again to its full height. About every second wave the children will have to take a step forward to give more slack in the parachute so it can continue to trap more air in the center, causing the igloo effect.

Every time the children wave the chute, it will go higher in the air on the upswing motion and not be lowered as far on the downward motion. After five or six waves the children will have built their dome-like igloo.

Standing in position, watch it settle to the ground. Have the children notice how far they moved to the center to build their igloo.

Build another igloo. This time when it is fully built, have the children look under the igloo and wave to a friend. Let it settle and walk it to its bunched up position.

Concluding Activity: Create another type of house, a tent. Have the children kneel around the bunched up chute. Have them get into the crawl position and drape the parachute over their backs and heads. Counting as they move, have them crawl two crawls forward and then stand up under the chute. They can build their tent by lifting their arms straight over their heads. Look around at friends. Whisper *"Hi"* to the people around them. Walk backwards from under the chute. Grab the edge immediately and lay it down.

Extension: Make a simple igloo or tent outside and enjoy activities in and around it.

GRAB THE BEANBAG

Suggested Units: Numbers

Additional Equipment: Bucket filled with beanbags, one beanbag for each child

Warm-Up Exercise: As the children gather around the bunched up chute, have them remain standing and grab it using the Thumbs-Down grip. Have them pretend they are window washers. They are going to wash all the windows on a ten floor building. Bend down with the chute to the first floor, jerk the chute back and forth several times as if to wash the windows. As the children wash, have them say, *"Swish, swish, swish."* Raise the chute slightly to the second floor, wash the windows, *"Swish, swish, swish."* Go up to the third floor and continue until the windows on all ten floors are washed. Have them slowly come back down to the ground level 10 - 9 - 8 - 7 - 6 - 5 - 4 - 3 - 2 - 1, and sit down. Explain the main activity and then walk the chute out.

Main Activity

Body Position: Standing

Hand Grip: Thumbs-Down (both hands)

Parachute Position: All areas

Parachute Motion: Taut

Directions: When the chute is fully spread out, have the children hold it using a Thumbs-Down grip, waist high. Then have the children count *"1, 2, 3, 4"* raising the chute to above their heads. When it is over their heads, give the bucket of bean-bags to a child. Have that child run under the chute, dump the beanbags in the middle of the area, give the teacher the empty bucket and then return to his place. When he grabs the chute, lower it *"4, 3, 2, 1"* back to waist high.

Now that the beanbags are in place, begin to play. The children around the chute are going to begin with the chute at their waist and count, *"1, 2, 3, 4"* gradually raising the chute above their head. When the chute is at its highest, the teacher should call out a child's name. That child lets go of the chute, runs or crawls to the center, grabs a beanbag, and goes back to his place on the chute. As the one child is going for the beanbag, the children begin lowering the chute as they count backwards, *"4, 3, 2, 1."* The child grabbing the beanbag tries to get back to his place before the chute is completely lowered. Continue, letting each child try to quickly grab a beanbag and get back to his place before the chute is lowered.

When everyone has a beanbag, have him pick it up. Walk the chute back to its bunched up position.

Concluding Activity: Have the children sit around the parachute. Bring the empty bucket out. One at a time have the children stand away from the bucket and toss the beanbag into it. After each child has tossed his beanbag into the bucket, he should leave the parachute area and go to his next activity.

Extension: Have the bucket and beanbags available for the children to use throughout the day.

55

WIGGLE WORM

Suggested Units: Spring, Creatures

Additional Equipment: Four foot long rope

Warm-Up Exercise: Have the children sit around the bunched up chute and grab it using the Thumbs-Up grip. Give them a series of rapid-fire commands.

- *"Hold the chute very tightly - STOP"*
- *"Hold the chute loosely - STOP"*
- *"Hold firmly, raise it high, wave it slowly - STOP"*
- *"Hold firmly, wave it slowly at your waist - STOP"*
- *"Hold firmly, wave it fast at your waist - STOP"*
- *"Hold it tight, jerk it five times - STOP"*

Continue. Just before the last command, explain the main activity.

- *"Stand up, hold the chute waist high and walk it out"*

Main Activity

Body Position: Sitting, kneeling, standing

Hand Grip: Thumbs-Up (two hands)

Parachute Position: Waist and knees

Parachute Motion: Snap, slow wave, jerk

Directions: The children should pretend that the rope is a worm. Give it to one of the children and have him put it on the parachute. Begin slowing waving the parachute and watch the worm wiggle. Is it moving very fast? Wave the chute a little faster. Now how is the worm moving? After a few more waving-wiggles change to the snapping motion. Try one snap. What did the worm do? Try several snaps in a row. How did the worm react? Change to the jerking motion. What kind of wiggling does the worm do when you jerk the chute?

Now that the children can move the worm using different motions, play Wiggle Worm. Pick three children who are standing next to each other around the parachute. Everyone is going to work together to wiggle the worm over to those children. First decide what motion you're going to use and how you will work together to get the worm to move in a specific direction. Now begin to wiggle the worm across the parachute. As the worm is moving, chant *"Wiggle, wiggle, wiggle worm"* over and over until the worm reaches the children. Pick three different children, use another motion, and wiggle the worm to those children. Continue playing Wiggle Worm until he has visited all of the children.

Concluding Activity: After all of this activity, the worm is pretty tired. Wiggle him gently toward the middle of the chute. With Wiggle Worm resting in the middle, walk the chute to its bunched up position.

Extension: Find worms outside. Watch how they wiggle.

 # SAY "HI"

Suggested Units: Self-Concept

Additional Equipment: None

Warm-Up Exercise: As the children gather around the parachute have them sit down. Enjoy this rhyme together.

FRIENDS

I say "Hello" to friends at school,
I'm happy as can be.
They are my special school friends
I like them all you see.

Then have each child stand up and the group say *"Hi, Elma."* Continue with the remaining children.

Discuss the different ways the children can say *"Hi"* to people using their body. Encourage them by creating various situations such as in a store, at a friend's house, etc.

After the discussion have them grab the chute with the Thumbs-Up grip and enjoy *"Where Is Thumbkin"* as described in Session II. Explain the main activity. Then help the children to re-arrange themselves around the chute so they are boy-girl as much as possible. Now grab the chute and walk it out.

Main Activity

Body Position: Standing

Hand Grip: Thumbs-Down

Parachute Position: Waist, over their heads

Parachute Motion: Taut

Directions: After the above discussion, have the children enjoy saying *"Hi"* to each other in many ways. Have them raise the chute over their heads.

- The teacher should call on two children. Say, *"John and Jim walk under the chute and say "Hi" by smiling at each other."*
- All the girls let go of the chute, walk three giant steps to the middle and bow. Walk back.
- Boys let go of the chute, walk two giant steps to the center and bow to each other. Walk back.
- Call on three children. Have them slide to the middle and wave to each other.
- Continue, using other ideas from the discussion.

In addition to having the children say *"Hi"* under the chute, vary the activity so the children can rest their arms by saying *"Hi"* in other ways. Lower the chute to their waist.

- Say *"Emma and Jim let go of the chute. Run around the chute until you meet. Pat each other on the back and run back to your places."*
- The children should hold the chute with one hand and shake hands with the person next to him.
- Continue, using more ideas from the children's discussion.

Concluding Activity: As the children walk the chute in, sing the song *"Hello"* by Ella Jenkins:

Hello, hello, hello and how are you?
I'm fine, I'm fine
I hope that you are too.

Extension: Make body silhouettes at art.

 # COOL OFF

Suggested Units: Summer, Air/Wind

Additional Equipment: One nylon scarf

Warm-Up Exercise: As the children arrive at the bunched up parachute, have them sit, stretch their legs under the chute and grab the edge using the Thumbs-Up grip. Have them slowly lift one leg counting *"1, 2, 3"* as they lift and then lower the leg counting backwards *"3, 2, 1."* Repeat with the other leg. After several leg lifts, have them turn around so they are sitting about a foot away from the edge of the chute with their backs toward it. They should lie down, grab the parachute with both hands, and pull it slightly over their heads. Hanging onto the chute, have them stretch their arms up high and bring them back low, stretch high and low. As they stretch their arms, they should call out, *"Stretch high, stretch low, stretch high, stretch low."*

After the children are warmed-up, have them sit around the chute and explain the main activity.

Main Activity

Body Position: Kneeling, standing

Hand Grip: Thumbs-Up

Parachute Position: Waist and over their head

Parachute Motion: Wave, jerk, flip-flop, snap

Directions: In this activity the children will be creating different amounts of wind under the parachute. They will also try to figure out which motion, speed, and position seems to create the most wind.

First have them stand and lift the chute up high. Call on a child to crawl under it, put the scarf in the middle, and crawl back out. Then pick two or three children to let go of the chute and sit down. They are going to be judges, watching the scarf and telling the others when it is not moving, moving a little, or moving alot. Their three key words are: *"No, little, alot."* As they play, change the judges often.

Begin moving the chute. Wave it very slowly. What do the judges say is happening to the scarf? Wave it quickly, high over their heads. Wave it low. Change to another motion. Now what do the judges say is happening to the scarf? Which motion caused more wind? Continue in this manner, always listening to the judges. In the end, try to determine which motion and speed caused the most and least amount of wind.

Concluding Activity: Have several children at a time crawl under the chute. They can rest lying down or sitting up. The children around the chute hold it waist high and move it slowly (use different motions), creating enough air to cool those who are resting under the chute. Change children and let several more cool off. Soon everyone will be relaxed. Walk the chute back in.

Extension: Have a display of toys and other things which create wind.

CATCH THE BALL

Suggested Units: Summer, Balls, Numbers

Additional Equipment: Beachball, large rubber ball, large sponge-type ball, beanbag

Warm-Up Exercise: When the children come to the bunched up parachute, have them grab it using the Thumbs-Down grip. Put the beachball on the chute. Have them walk it out, being careful to keep the ball on the chute.

When it is fully spread out, put the beachball in the middle. Together begin snapping the chute causing the ball to fly in the air. Keep snapping in unison to bounce the ball. Once the children have a feel for the rhythm, stop. When they begin again, have them count how many times the beachball bounces before it goes off the chute. Switch to another type of ball. Practice and then have the children count how many times they can bounce this ball before it flies off. Repeat with the other ball and then the beanbag. Which was the easiest to keep on the chute? Hardest?

Everyone sit down. Explain the main activity.

Main Activity

Body Position: Standing

Hand Grip: Thumbs-Up

Parachute Position: Waist

Parachute Motion: Long, slow wave

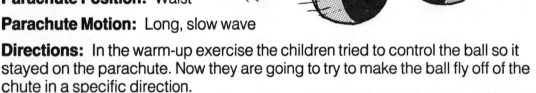

Directions: In the warm-up exercise the children tried to control the ball so it stayed on the parachute. Now they are going to try to make the ball fly off of the chute in a specific direction.

Have one child let go of the chute and move three or four giant steps backwards. Put one of the balls onto the chute. Have the children around the chute begin to wave it slowly. After several waves, wave the ball to the farside of the chute. Everyone say *"1, 2, 3, Toss."* As the group says *"Toss"* the children on that side of the chute should give the chute a hard upward swing so the ball flies off the chute toward the catcher on the outside of the chute. The child standing off of the chute should catch the ball, toss it back onto the chute, and take his place again on the chute. Another child should drop off of the chute to catch the ball. Continue until all of the children have had a chance to be the catcher. The last person should put the ball away.

Concluding Activity: Have the children use giant steps when they walk the chute back to its bunched up position. Count the steps as they walk. Walk the chute back out. Walk it in again, this time using regular steps. Again count. Walk it out once more. This time walk the chute in using very short steps. Count. Which way took the most steps? Least? Which way did they like best?

Extension: Enjoy sponge painting with small sponge-type balls.

PARACHUTE CATCH

Suggested Units: Summer, Toys, Balls

Additional Equipment: Beachball or large rubber ball, piece of colored chalk

Warm-Up Exercise: Have the children sit in a wide circle without the bunched up chute in the middle. Give one child the ball. Have him call out another child's name and then roll it to that child. When he catches it, he calls on another child and rolls it to that child. Continue playing catch for a while.

Now have the children stand. Continue playing catch as described above, but bounce the ball to each other.

After playing catch without the parachute, bring the chute out. Have the children sit around it and explain the activity. Then stand. Grab the chute Thumbs-Down and walk it out. As they walk, have them snap the chute. Chant *"Snap"* at each movement. When fully out, have them keep snapping in rhythm until they hear *"Stop."*

Main Activity

Body Position: Standing

Hand Grip: Thumbs-Down

Parachute Position: Waist

Parachute Motion: Hard snap

Directions: When the chute is fully spread out, the teacher should mark the middle of the chute with a chalk line. While doing this, s/he should tell the children that the chalk line divides the parachute in half or in two sections.

Divide the children in half so they are standing around the chute on each side of the chalk line.

Toss the ball onto one side of the chute. Now the children are going to play Parachute Catch. Using the snapping motion, the children on one side should snap the chute causing the ball to fly over to the other side. (Use several snaps if necessary.) The children on the other side of the chute simply lower the chute a little causing the ball to be caught. Then they snap the ball back to the other side. Those children catch the ball and snap it back.

After playing Parachute Catch, roll the ball back and forth across the line. Each time make the ball roll a little slower. Finally, it goes so slowly, that it stops. Walk the chute to the middle and sit down around it.

Concluding Activity: Enjoy these ryhmes about balls.

HERE'S A BALL

Here's a ball,
And here's a ball
A great big ball I see

Shall we count them?
Are you ready?
One, two, three!

I'M BOUNCING

I'm bouncing, bouncing everywhere.
I bounce and bounce into the air.
I'm bouncing, bouncing like a ball.
I bounce and bounce, then down I fall.

Extension: Have all sizes of balls on the playground. Encourage the children to play catch.

FLOATING THE CHUTE

Suggested Units: Self-Concept, Body Awareness

Additional Equipment: None

Warm-Up Exercise: When the children gather around the bunched up chute, have them remain standing and grab it using the Thumbs-Up grip. Have the children slowly tighten their hold on the parachute counting *"1, 2, 3, 4, 5."* Pause and then slowly loosen their grip as they count backwards *"5, 4, 3, 2, 1."* Relax. Repeat this several times and then walk the chute out to its fully spread position.

The children should remain standing and grab the chute using the Thumbs-Up grip. This time have them hold on tightly, keep their feet flat on the floor, and lean back, pulling on the chute, counting *"1, 2, 3, 4, 5."* Pause and slowly straighten up as they count *"5, 4, 3, 2, 1."* Repeat this in a kneeling and sitting position.

While sitting, explain the main activity.

Main Activity

Body Position: Sitting, kneeling, standing

Hand Grip: Thumbs-Up

Parachute Position: Knees, waist, over the head

Parachute Motion: Very taut

Directions: The children are going to learn two different ways to make the parachute float. In the first way have the children stand, grab the chute with the Thumbs-Up grip, and hold it at their knees. Slowly they should raise the chute above their heads. As they do, chant, *"Higher, higher, higher, higher,"* and at the top, *"Highest."* When they say *"Highest"* they should let the chute go and watch it float to the ground. Do it several times from the standing position. Kneel and try it. Sit and try it again. Which is the most exciting? Did the parachute float straight down? Did it land all spread out and flat?

Remain sitting to learn the second way. Have the children grab the chute, Thumbs-Up. They will need to hold on very tightly, just as they did in the warm-up exercise. Holding on, have the children all pull back on the chute, counting *"1, 2, 3, 4, 5."* After saying *"5"* they should whisper *"Float."* When they say *"Float"* they should all let go of the chute together. The chute will jerk a little and float to the ground. Try it again. Change to the kneeling and standing positions and enjoy floating the chute.

Concluding Activity: From a standing position, float the chute the first way. This time, as it is coming down, grab it when it is about waist high. Walk it to its bunched-up position.

Extension: Make an on-going list of everything you can think of that floats. Tack it on a wall for everyone to use.

63

 **BODY PARTS**

Suggested Units: Body Awareness

Additional Equipment: None

Warm-Up Exercise: Have the children sit around the bunched up parachute with their legs stretched out under it. Grab the chute with both hands, using a Thumbs-Down grip. Now have them bend forward and touch their knees with their hands, sit back up; touch their ankles, sit up; touch their toes, sit up. Use a Thumbs-Up grip and repeat.

Explain the main activity, stand up, and walk the chute out until it is fully open.

Main Activity

Body Position: Standing

Hand Grip: Thumbs-Up or Thumbs-Down (both hands)

Parachute Position: All Areas

Parachute Motion: Taut

Directions: Have the children hold the parachute taut. The teacher calls out a specific body part and the children move the chute up or down so that it is even with the named part. When everyone has the parachute in place, the group says, *"We're pointing to our knees"* or whatever body part it is.

Continue the activity naming both large and small body parts. Once the children understand how to play, let them take turns calling out body parts.

For added excitement, speed up the calling and do not have the group repeat the name of the designated body part. One caller simply gives rapid fire directions.

When the group tires, have them put the chute down and sit around it. Repeat the warm-up exercise in slow motion and then crawl or scoot the chute back to its bunched up position.

Concluding Activity: When the chute is back, enjoy the following rhyme.

BODY BAND

Beat, beat with your feet,
We're playing the body band.

Strum, strum with your thumb,
It's the best one in the land.

Clap, clap on your lap,
Keep rhythm with your knees.

Hear, hear with your ear,
Stop laughing if you please.

Cluck, cluck like a duck,
It's fun on a rainy day.

Pop, pop on your top,
Keep humming as you play.

Moan, moan all alone,
You're playing your solo now.

Haste, haste with your waist,
It's time to take your bow!

Dick Wilmes

Extension: For snacks enjoy some gingerbread cookies cut in the shape of people.

# KITE FLYING

Suggested Units: Spring, Air/Wind, Toys

Additional Equipment: Marker

Warm-Up Exercise: When the children gather around the bunched up chute, mark an X on their right hand and an O on their left one. Then using a Thumbs-Up grip, have them walk the chute out and sit down with their legs stretched out underneath the chute. Grab the chute very tightly with the Thumbs-Up grip and pull back as hard as they can, counting *"1, 2, 3,"* and relax. Pull back again, count, and relax. Repeat this exercise while kneeling, and then standing, holding the parachute at their waist and then over their head. After exercising, have the children carry the chute outside.

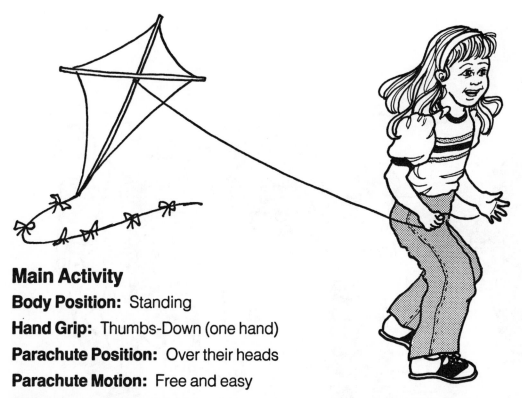

Main Activity

Body Position: Standing

Hand Grip: Thumbs-Down (one hand)

Parachute Position: Over their heads

Parachute Motion: Free and easy

Directions: This activity should be enjoyed outside or in a large room such as a gym or an activity center.

Have all of the children stand close together on one side of the parachute. (If your group is too large, use half on the chute, while the other half chants this song to the tune of *"Row, Row, Row Your Boat."*

Fly, fly, fly your kite
Fly it up and down,
Flying, flying, flying, flying
Flying all around.

Dick Wilmes

Have them grab the parachute with the X (right) hand, using the Thumbs-Down grip. When everyone is ready, say, *"Let's fly our kite!"* All of the children begin to slowly jog in the same direction. As they gain a little more speed, they should raise their arms higher and higher. This will help lift the parachute and let it fly like a kite. As they are moving, have them look back and see how the parachute is flapping in the wind.

Direct them to make wide sweeping turns, all moving in the same direction. To do this, they'll need to slow down and some will almost have to stop until everyone on the outside of the turn has gotten around. Fly the 'kite' back to the beginning spot and rest. While resting, talk about this new type of kite.

If they are not too tired, continue the 'kite flying.' This time have them grab the parachute with the O (left) hand, using the Thumbs-Up grip.

Once they can control their new 'kite,' vary the activity slightly. As they are running with the chute, have the children wave it by slowly raising and lowering their arms. This waving motion will cause the 'kite' to flap up and down as it flies. Once again rest.

Concluding Activity: As they are flying the 'kite' back to the starting point for the last time, have them move slower and make several giant up and down movements with their arms. They will notice the chute rise and fall as they do this. Gather up the parachute and bring it inside.

Extension: Make small paper kites as an art activity.

🌂 FLOATING CLOUDS

Suggested Units: Weather, Clouds

Additional Equipment: None

Warm-Up Exercise: Have the children sit around the bunched up chute. Read this riddle and let them guess what the rhyme is describing.

What's fluffy white and floats up high,
Like piles of ice cream in the sky?
And when the wind blows hard and strong,
What very gently floats along?

What seems to have just lots of fun,
Peek-a-booing with the sun?
When you look up in the big blue sky,
What are these things floating by?

When they guess *"clouds"* tell them that today they are going to transform the parachute into a cloud. Explain the activity. Then have them grab the parachute with both hands, using the Thumbs-Down grip. Walk the chute out, raising their arms up, up, up as they walk. When it is fully spread out, the chute will be over their heads.

Main Activity

Body Position: Standing

Hand Grip: Thumbs-Down (one hand)

Parachute Position: All areas

Parachute Motion: Taut

Directions: This activity should be done outside or in a large room such as a gym or an activity center.

Have the children lay the fully spread out chute on the ground and sit down. While resting, talk about clouds—sometimes they float high in the sky, other times they are so low you could almost touch them. Sometimes they move across the sky ever so slowly, yet other times there is a strong wind and they go speeding across.

Now that the children's arms are rested, have them stand and grab the chute with two hands, using the Thumbs-Down grip. Raise it high over their heads and walk in one direction. As they walk, the air under the chute will create a shallow rippling effect similar to a slowly floating cloud.

Change direction, 'float' the parachute using only one hand. Everyone grab the chute with his inside hand, Thumbs-Down grip, and raise it high. This time, walk a little faster for the breeze is beginning to blow harder.

As the group continues to float the cloud, have them walk quickly, raise it high, and bring it down low.

Concluding Activity: Change speed to create a very lazy, slow moving cloud. Soon this slow moving cloud has no more breeze to help it float along and it disappears. Have the children walk the chute into its bunched up position.

Extension: Read the book It Looked Like Spilt Milk by George Shaw.

PARACHUTE GOLF

Suggested Units: Buildings, Families

Additional Equipment: Wiffle or small rubber ball - appropriate size to fit through the hole in the center of the chute, a piece of posterboard with the numbers 1-9 written across the top, marker

Warm-Up Exercise: The children should remain standing as they come to the bunched up chute and grab it with the Thumbs-Up grip. Have them use the flip-flop motion as they walk backwards spreading out the chute.

When it is fully out, wave the chute in a variety of ways:

- Slow, steady waves
- Slow, very long waves

Continue

- Quick, short waves
- Slow, short waves
- Quick, long waves

- Wave slowly to the ground and sit down. Explain the main activity.

Main Activity

Body Position: Standing

Hand Grip: Thumbs-Up (both hands)

Parachute Position: Mainly waist

Parachute Motion: Wave or snap

1	2	3	4	5	6	7	8	9
3	6	2						

Directions: Using a waving motion the children will try to get the ball through the hole in the middle of the chute.

Before they can go to the 'golf course,' however, they must practice on the 'putting green.' Toss the ball onto the chute. Begin waving it, trying to maneuver the ball through the hole. When the ball is sunk, have someone retrieve it and toss it back onto the chute.

After the children have had enough practice, they should go to the 'golf course.' Bring out the scorecard marked one through nine. This time the children have to count how many strokes it takes them to make a hole. (A stroke is any shot toward the hole.)

Toss the ball onto the chute. The children begin counting their strokes aloud as they wave the ball towards the hole. When they sink the ball, write the number of strokes on the scorecard. Continue to the second, third, fourth, and on through the ninth hole.

When they are finished, have them flip-flop the chute as they walk it in. Sit around the bunched up parachute.

Concluding Activity: Talk about the scorecard. How many strokes did it take them at the first hole? On which hole did they use the least number of strokes? The most?

Extension: Hang the scorecard in a place where everyone can easily see it. Talk about it often. Use it again when you play Parachute Golf.

 **TAG**

Suggested Units: Body Awareness

Additional Equipment: Drum, marker

Warm-Up Exercise: When the children gather around the bunched up chute, have them stand. Quickly go around the chute and mark an X on the children's right hands and an O on their left ones. Then have them grab the chute with both hands using the Thumbs-Down grip, and run backwards until it is fully spread out. Begin giving them directions. After each direction, start beating a drum, so they know what speed to move and when to start and stop.

- *"Jog to the X"* (right) - beat very slowly
- *"Run to the O"* (left) - beat medium speed
- *"Jog to the O"* - beat slowly for a short time
- *"Run to the X"* - beat fast for a short time

Continue changing directions, speeds, and length of time.

- *"Sit down."* Explain the main activity.

Main Activity

Body Position: Standing

Hand Grip: Thumbs-Down

Parachute Position: Over their head

Parachute Motion: Fairly taut

Directions: The children should stand evenly spaced around the chute. The teacher should pick two children, instructing one to chase the other. *"Sally, you will chase Ryan."* Those two children should drop off of the chute, while the other children raise it over their heads. When the teacher signals *"Go,"* Sally begins to run after Ryan. The two children must stay near the chute. They can run under the chute, between the children, or around the immediate periphery of the chute. If Sally catches Ryan or if the chase lasts several minutes, the teacher signals *"Stop."* Lower the chute and the teacher picks two more children. Raise the chute and *"Go"* again.

Continue until everyone has played Tag.

Concluding Activity: Have the children lay the chute on the ground, kneel around it, and grab it with both hands. When the teacher says *"Go"* the children should bunch up the chute by grabbing the material of the parachute in their hands as they crawl towards the middle. When the chute is all bunched up, sit and rest for several minutes.

Extension: Enjoy various forms of tag while playing outside.

BUG IN MY CHUTE

Suggested Units: Spring, Bugs

Additional Equipment: None

Warm-Up Exercise: Have the children grab the bunched up chute, Thumbs-Up, and walk it out. Then have them hold it high above their heads. Enjoy exercising under the parachute. The teacher gives directions. Remember to rest when necessary.

- *"Sally and Sam, change places by running under the chute to each other's place."*
- *"Ian, go to the middle and jump up and down four times. We'll count for you."*
- *"Manda, do a sommersault under the chute."*

Continue.

- *"Everyone sit down and lay the chute on the ground."* Teach the children the rhyme and then explain the main activity.

Main Activity

Body Position: Kneeling

Hand Grip: Thumbs-Up

Parachute Position: Waist high

Parachute Motion: Taut

Directions: The children should kneel around the chute, grabbing it with a Thumbs-Up grip. Say the rhyme several times:

Bug in my chute
Bug in my chute
Who is that bug in my chute?

Once the children are familiar with the rhyme, have them hold the chute up a little bit and tightly close their eyes. While the children's eyes are closed, walk around the chute. Pick a child to crawl under the chute. When the child is under, have the others open their eyes and say the rhyme. As they are saying the rhyme, they should be looking around the chute and figuring out who is missing. When they think they know, have them call out the child's name. Have the child under the chute slowly crawl out. Were they right? Enjoy again and again!!

When finished, walk the chute to the middle and stand around it.

Concluding Activity: Think of a bug and how it moves. As the children leave the parachute, have them move like that bug.

Extension: Look for different bugs outside. How many can they find? How do the bugs move?

70

# ROW YOUR BOAT

Suggested Units: Summer, Water Fun, Transportation

Additional Equipment: Several favorite musical records

Warm-Up Exercise: Have a record playing as they come to the bunched up chute. Let them grab the chute, Thumbs-Down, and start dancing in place to the beat of the music. Change the song to one with a different beat and let them continue dancing. After a while, stop the music, have them sit around the bunched up chute and explain the main activity.

Begin playing the music again and let them dance as they bring the chute out. When fully out, dance for a little while, then turn off the music and have the children sit down.

Main Activity

Body Position: Sitting

Hand Grip: Thumbs-Down (two hands)

Parachute Position: Waist

Parachute Motion: Various speeds of waving

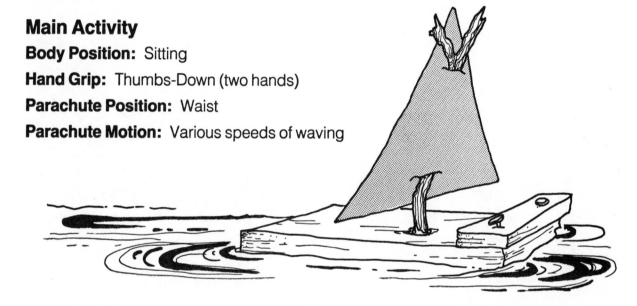

Directions: In the beginning they will sing *"Row, Row, Row Your Boat"* at its regular speed, while waving the parachute in rhythm. As the group is singing the song, have one child pretend to row a boat around the (parachute) lake. He should walk around the parachute moving his arms in a rowing motion. After rowing for a little while, he should stop behind another child. That child then gets up and begins to row. The first child takes his new place on the chute and begins to wave it with the group.

The next time you play the game, have the children wave the chute and sing at different speeds. The person rowing must listen to the song and watch the chute to know the speed at which he should be rowing.

Concluding Activity: Wave the chute and sing as you walk the chute to its bunched up position.

Extension: Have small boats in the water table.

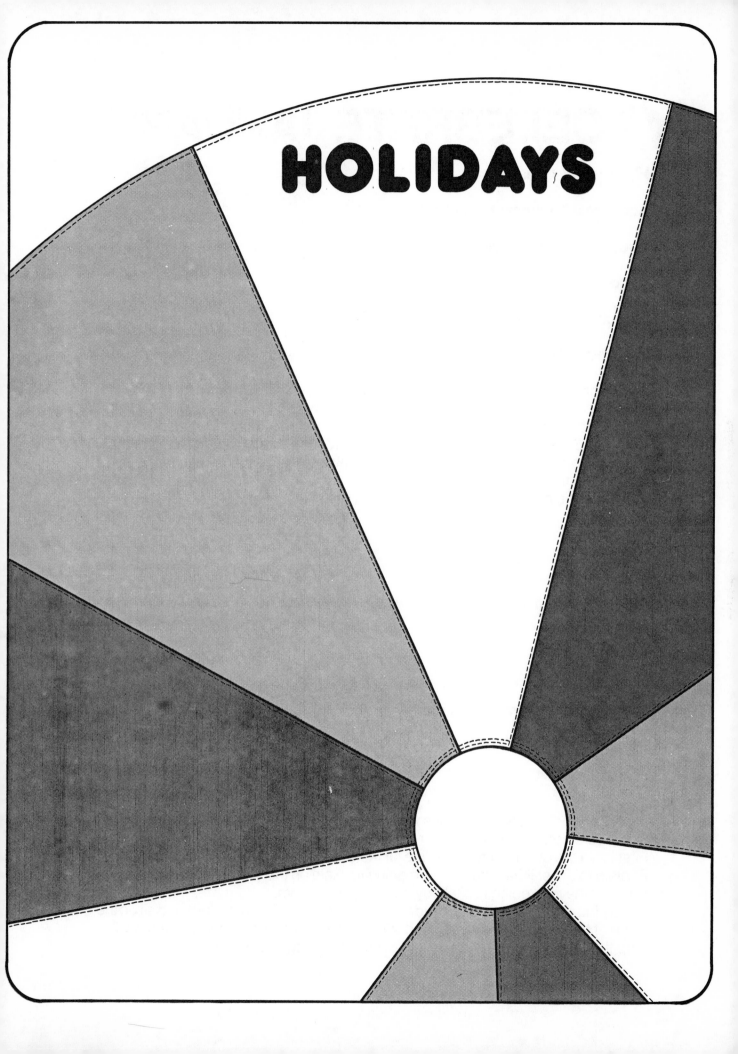

CELEBRATE JANUARY

Happy New Year

Additional Equipment: Balloons

Body Position: Standing

Hand Grip: Thumbs-Up

Parachute Position: Waist, over their heads

Parachute Motion: Snap, wave

Directions: Sit around the parachute and slowly count backwards from 10 to 1. After the children say *"1,"* all shout *"Happy New Year!"*

Now stand. Hold onto the chute with a Thumbs-Up grip. Slowly count backwards —*"10, 9, 8, 7, 6, 5, 4, 3, 2, 1."* As the children say each number have them give the chute a giant snap. As they shout *"Happy New Year"* have them wave the chute in unison into the giant mushroom shape.

Repeat the activity with balloons on the chute.

Ice Skating

Additional Equipment: Instrumental music

Body Position: Sitting, crawling

Hand Grip: None

Parachute Position: Flat on floor

Parachute Motion: Taut

Directions: Talk about the times when the children have been ice skating or have watched others ice skate. Then pretend that the parachute is an ice skating rink. First have the children touch the 'ice.' It feels slippery. Talk about ice for awhile. Explain to the children that they are going to skate on the 'ice.' Because it is very slippery they are going to skate by crawling on all fours.

Play the music. Tap several children to begin skating. The others should sit on the edge of the chute to keep it taut and sway to the rhythm of the music. After awhile stop the music, change skaters, and continue skating and swaying.

 # CELEBRATE FEBRUARY

Heart Match

Additional Equipment: Matching felt hearts of different sizes, felt board

Body Position: Standing

Hand Grip: Thumbs-Up

Parachute Position: Waist, over their heads

Parachute Motion: Taut

Directions: Match the hearts on the felt board before using the parachute. Talk about the different sizes. Now mix the hearts up and give them to several children.

Have the children stand, grab the chute with the Thumbs-Up grip, and raise the chute over their heads. The children holding the hearts should run under the chute and spread the hearts in the center, then run out and grab the chute. Lower the chute to waist high. Now the game is set up.

Have the children again raise the chute above their heads, call on one or two children. Those children run under the chute, look for a matching pair of hearts, and run out. They should put the matching hearts on the felt board and return to the chute. Repeat until all of the hearts are on the felt board.

Shadows

Additional Equipment: Large flashlight

Body Position: Lying down

Hand Grip: None

Parachute Position: On the floor

Parachute Motion: None

Directions: Have all of the children pretend that they are ground hogs hibernating in their holes, by lying on the floor under the edge of the chute. As they are hibernating, tell them the legend of how the ground hog looks for his shadow.

Tap a child on the shoulder. This is his signal to come out of his 'hole' and look for his shadow. He can go over to a shining light, discover his shadow, and run back to his 'hole' or keep looking and never find his shadow. Continue by tapping each 'ground hog' and letting him look for his shadow.

🪂 CELEBRATE MARCH

Who Is Patrick?

Additional Equipment: None

Body Position: Sitting

Hand Grip: Thumbs-Down

Parachute Position: About one foot off the floor

Parachute Motion: Taut

Directions: While the children are playing this game, they will need to remember that leprechauns are very quiet, sneaky, and secretive.

Have all of the children sit around the chute, grab it with a Thumbs-Down grip, and raise it slightly off of the ground. Everyone should close his eyes. Walk around the chute and tap someone to be Patrick. That child crawls under the chute to the middle. Then he pokes a part of his body (elbow, arm, foot, knee) through the hole. The other children open their eyes, look at the part of Patrick peeking through the hole, and try to guess who is Patrick. After guessing, Patrick crawls out. Enjoy again and again.

 # CELEBRATE APRIL

Bunny Hop

Additional Equipment: Music for the song *"Bunny Hop"*

Body Position: Standing

Hand Grip: Thumbs-Up

Parachute Position: Waist

Parachute Motion: Wave or flip-flop

Directions: Standing around the chute, have the children enjoy doing the *"Bunny Hop"* without holding the parachute.

Once they understand the basic dance, have them grab the chute with the Thumbs-Up grip. Holding the chute, let them begin to dance. When the music indicates the *"hop, hop, hop,"* have the children hop towards the middle. After several sequences, the children will be in a tight circle. Continue dancing, only now, *"hop, hop, hop"* backwards.

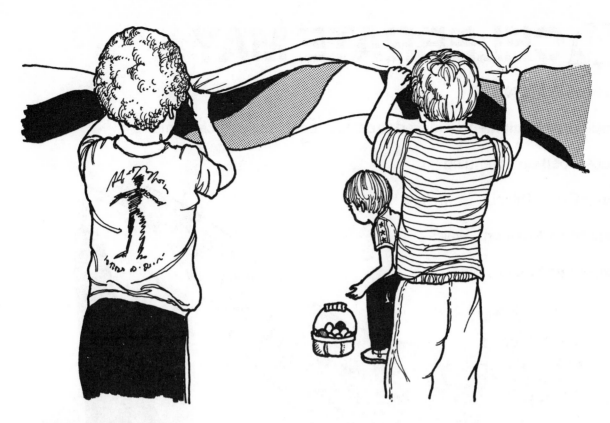

Colored Egg Hunt

Additional Equipment: Colored, plastic eggs filled with raisins and nuts, basket

Body Position: Standing

Hand Grip: Thumbs-Down

Parachute Position: Waist, over their heads

Parachute Motion: Taut

Directions: Bring the basket filled with plastic eggs to the parachute. Hold up each egg and have the children call out the color of the egg. When finished have the children grab the parachute with the Thumbs-Down grip and raise it over their heads. Have a child put the basket under the chute. Now the game is set up.

To play, have the children raise the chute, call on a child to run under the chute, grab a certain color egg, and then run out. Lower the chute. Repeat until everyone has an egg. When parachute play is over, the children can enjoy the snack hiding in each egg.

Variation: Instead of using a basket of eggs, put the Seder plate with pictures of the traditional foods on it under the middle of the chute. As the chute is raised, call on a child to go under the chute and take a specific picture of food off of the plate, and run back out. When the chute is lowered, talk about the symbolism of the food.

 # CELEBRATE MAY

Maypole March

Additional Equipment: Colored streamers, beachball, marching music

Body Position: Standing

Hand Grip: Thumbs-Down (one hand)

Parachute Position: Waist

Parachute Motion: Wave

Directions: The teacher will create a Maypole by standing under the middle of the chute and holding the beachball high in the air.

As each child comes to the parachute, give him a colored streamer and let him loosely tape it to the edge of the chute. Have the children grab the chute with one hand and raise it waist high. The teacher should go under the chute and raise the middle up. Have someone begin the music. The children march in the same direction waving their decorated 'Maypole.' As the children are marching, the teacher can give various special directions such as, *"If you like red flowers, let go of the chute and come under the 'Maypole.'"* In a little while say *"Those children who like red flowers, grab onto the chute again."* Give other special directions as the children are enjoying their Maypole March.

Extension: Have sponge balls the children can roll back and forth inside.

 # CELEBRATE JUNE

Where Are The Bees?

Additional Equipment: None

Body Position: Kneeling

Hand Grip: Thumbs-Up

Parachute Position: About two feet off the floor

Parachute Motion: Slow flip-flop

Directions: First teach the children this rhyme:

BEEHIVE

Here is the beehive
Where are the bees?
Hidden away where nobody sees.
Soon they come creeping out of the hive
One, two, three, four, five.

Have everyone kneel down and grab the chute with the Thumbs-Up grip. Flip-flop the chute slowly. As the children move the chute, tell them that they are going to pretend that the parachute is a beehive. There are lots of bees in the 'hive' and it is wiggling.

Then call on four or five children to crawl under the chute and pretend that they are the bees in the 'hive.' When all of the bees are in the 'hive,' the remaining children say the rhyme as they gently move the 'hive.' Instead of counting on the last line, call one bee's name. That bee creeps out. Continue until all of the bees are out of the 'hive.' Enjoy several times.

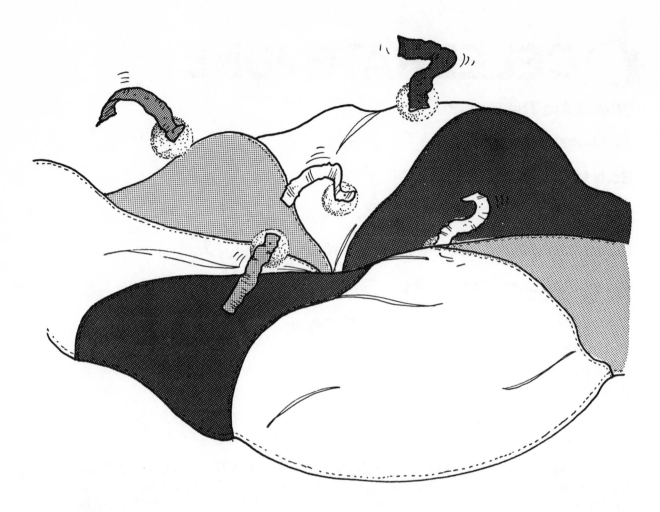

Old Glory

Additional Equipment: A recording of Sousa marches, white styrofoam balls with red and blue streamers attached

Body Position: Standing

Hand Grip: Thumbs-Up (one hand)

Parachute Position: Waist

Parachute Motion: Wave

Directions: Have the children hold the parachute with both hands. Play the recording and let them march in place to the beat of the music.

   After they have marched for awhile, stop the music. Let the children toss the decorated balls onto the chute. Holding the chute with one hand, begin the music, and have the children march in one direction, waving the chute as they do. The waving motion of the chute will cause the streamers to fly in the air like gently moving flags.

CELEBRATE JULY

Tug-Tug-Tug

Additional Equipment: None

Body Position: Standing

Hand Grip: Fist

Parachute Position: Waist

Parachute Motion: Parachute is rolled up

Directions: July is picnic time. Play a picnic game with the parachute. Have the children all kneel on one side of the parachute and slowly roll it up until it makes a rope.

Now divide the group into two teams. Have the teams grab opposite ends of the 'rope.' To play Tug-Tug-Tug, one team pulls and the second team holds back. Then switch. The second team pulls and the first team holds back. Each side should have the chance to tug and hold back. Switch teams and play again. This time have the team chant *"Tug, tug, tug"* as they pull back.

Dunk Tank

Additional Equipment: Pail, 10-12 tennis balls

Body Position: Standing or kneeling

Hand Grip: Thumbs-Up

Parachute Position: Waist

Parachute Motion: Wave

Directions: Have the children sit around the stretched out chute and hold it taut with the Thumbs-Up grip. Give one child the pail. Have him crawl under the chute and put the pail under the hole. Toss a tennis ball onto the chute. Have the children wave the chute trying to dunk the ball through the hole so it lands in the 'tank.' Continue dunking all the balls. When all of the balls have been dunked, count how many balls landed in the 'tank' and how many missed.

# CELEBRATE AUGUST

Happy Birthday

Additional Equipment: Balloons

Body Position: Standing

Hand Grip: Thumbs-Up

Parachute Position: Waist

Parachute Motion: Snap, wave, mushroom, flip-flop, jerk

Directions: Have the children put the balloons on the parachute and snap the chute as they sing *"Happy Birthday."* Sing again while waving the chute. Use different motions and sing again and again. When finished, hang the balloons from the ceiling.

How Old Are You?

Additional Equipment: None

Body Position: Standing

Hand Grip: Thumbs-Up

Parachute Position: Waist

Parachute Motion: Snap

Directions: Have the children stand and grab the chute with a Thumbs-Up grip. Pretend that it is each child's birthday. Call on a child. That child tells the others his real age or an age he would like to be. Then the children snap the chute the appropriate number of times, counting aloud as they snap. When finished, everyone looks at the birthday child and says *"Happy Birthday, Raul."* Ask another child how old he is today. Continue until everyone has celebrated a birthday.

# CELEBRATE SEPTEMBER

Old McDonald Had A Farm

Additional Equipment: None

Body Position: Standing

Hand Grip: Thumbs-Up

Parachute Position: Over their heads, waist

Parachute Motion: Jerk, taut

Directions: While sitting around the chute, sing the song *"Old McDonald Had A Farm."* Talk about all of the work a farmer does.

Now have the children stand and grab the chute with a Thumbs-Up grip. Everyone sing the song and slowly jerk the chute. When the children sing the animal sound, quickly raise the chute, have a child go under the chute and act like that animal. When finished with the animal sound, the child runs back out, and the group lowers the chute and continues to sing about another animal.

Apple Seed

Additional Equipment: None

Body Position: All positions

Hand Grip: Thumbs-Down

Parachute Position: All positions

Parachute Motion: Taut

Directions: Create an apple tree with the children. Turn off the lights and have the children curl up as small as possible and put the edge of the chute over them as if covered by the ground. Thus they are the apple seeds waiting to sprout. With enough water and sunlight (turn on the lights) the apple seeds begin to grow (have the children peek out and squat holding the chute). They continue to grow (children raise the chute a little higher) until they are a full grown apple tree (children stand and put the chute high over their heads).

While the chute is over their heads enjoy this rhyme together.

APPLE TREE

Way up high in the apple tree,
Two little apples smiled at me,
I shook that tree as hard as I could,
Down came the apples,
Umm, Umm, Good!

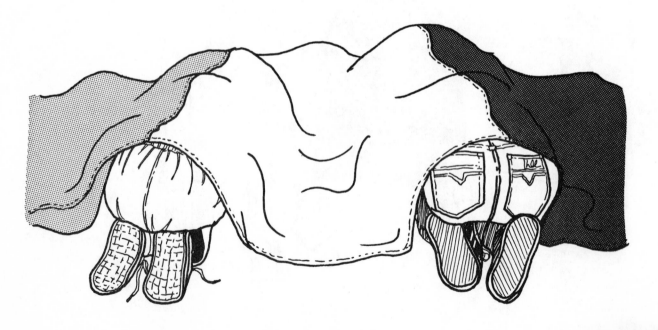

CELEBRATE OCTOBER

Haunted House

Additional Equipment: None

Body Position: Standing

Hand Grip: Thumbs-Up

Parachute Position: Off the floor, over their heads

Parachute Motion: Taut, mushroom

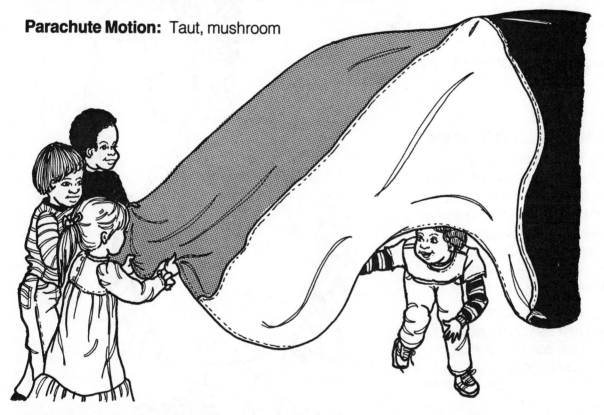

Directions: Have all of the children think of a character that they would like to pretend to be in a haunted house. Have each child tell the group what his character is and then act like it. When everyone has told about his character, have the children stand and grab the parachute with a Thumbs-Up grip. The parachute is going to be a 'haunted house.'

Have the children bend down and hold the chute close to the floor. Call on a child to crawl into the 'haunted house.' While in the 'haunted house' the child can act and sound like his character. Then all of a sudden the children around the chute open the 'haunted house' door by mushrooming the chute. When the chute is up they say *"Boo!"* The child under the chute stands up, makes a scary face, and runs out of the 'haunted house.' Continue, using other characters.

# CELEBRATE NOVEMBER

Run Fast Little Turkey

Additional Equipment: None

Body Position: Sitting

Hand Grip: Thumbs-Up

Parachute Position: Off the floor

Parachute Motion: Wave, flip-flop

Directions: First teach the children this rhyme:

RUN FAST LITTLE TURKEY

The brave little Pilgrim
Went out in the wood.
Looking for a meal
That would taste really good.

First he picked cranberries
Out in a bog.
Then he saw a turkey
Hiding in a log.

Run fast little turkey,
Run fast as you may,
Or you'll come to dinner
On Thanksgiving Day.
                    Dick Wilmes

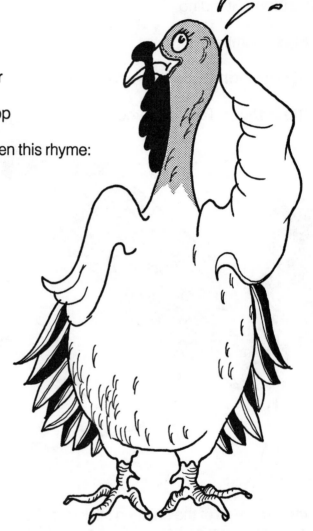

When the children know the rhyme, have them sit around a spread out chute. Pick one child to be the Pilgrim. He begins to walk around the parachute looking for foods as the others slowly wave the chute and say the first two verses of the rhyme. As the children say *"Then he saw a turkey, hiding in a log,"* point to another child who is the turkey. That child gets up and begins to quickly run around the chute. The Pilgrim chases him. During the chase the children flip-flop the chute and say the last verse of the rhyme. If the turkey gets back to his place, he's safe. If he is caught, he must sit in the middle of the chute.

Pass The Hat

Additional Equipment: A Pilgrim hat for each child

Body Position: Standing

Hand Grip: Thumbs-Down

Parachute Position: Waist

Parachute Motion: Taut

Directions: First learn this song, sung to the tune of *"Row, Row, Row Your Boat."*

Pass, pass, pass the hat
Pass it 'round and 'round.
Passing, passing, passing, passing,
Quickly 'til it's found.

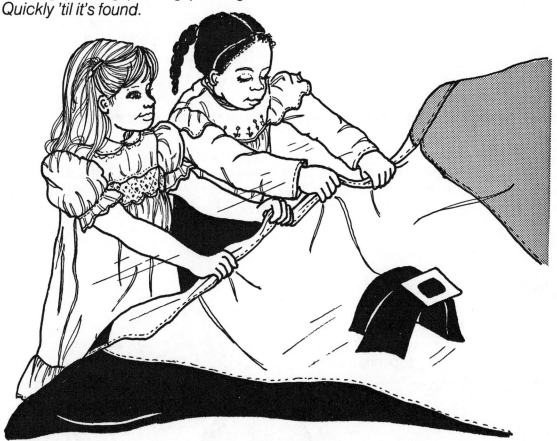

    Grab the chute with a Thumbs-Down grip and hold it taut. Begin passing the chute around and around, singing the song. After singing the song several times, put a Pilgrim hat on the edge of the chute. Sing again and pass the chute around. Stop the chute after singing the rhyme one time. The person near the hat should take the hat off of the chute and put it on. Place another Pilgrim hat on the chute. Sing again. Continue until all of the children become Pilgrims.

# CELEBRATE DECEMBER

Find Your Shoes

Additional Equipment: None

Body Position: Standing

Hand Grip: Thumbs-Up

Parachute Position: Waist, over their heads

Parachute Motion: Mushroom

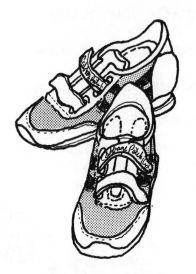

Directions: First have the children take off their shoes. (Talk about how some children get presents in their shoes.) One at a time, have each child crawl under the chute and put his pair of shoes in the middle.

When all of the shoes are under the chute, have the children stand and grab it with the Thumbs-Up grip. Then call on a child. Have the others mushroom the chute. The named child should run under the chute, find his pair of shoes, and run back out again. Have each child find his pair of shoes.

Jingle Bells

Additional Equipment: Bells, recording of *"Jingle Bells"* (optional)

Body Position: Standing

Hand Grip: Thumbs-Up

Parachute Position: Waist

Parachute Motion: Jerk

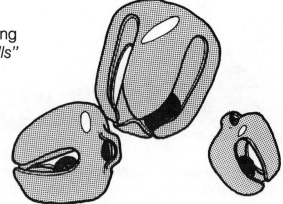

Directions: Give each child several bells. Let them toss their bells onto the chute and sing *"Jingle Bells"* as they jerk the chute in rhythm to their singing and dancing. If you have a recording of *"Jingle Bells,"* play the music and shake the bells.

Wrapping Gifts

Additional Equipment: Small toy for each child

Body Position: Sitting

Hand Grip: None

Parachute Position: On the floor

Parachute Motion: Taut

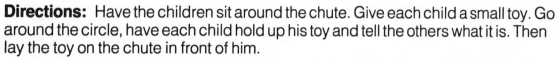

Directions: Have the children sit around the chute. Give each child a small toy. Go around the circle, have each child hold up his toy and tell the others what it is. Then lay the toy on the chute in front of him.

After everyone has told about his toy, have the group cover their eyes. Tap one child on the head. That child should wrap his toy in the parachute. Have the children uncover their eyes and see if they can remember what gift just got wrapped up. After several guesses let the child unwrap his toy so everyone can see it.

Snow Angels

Additional Equipment: None

Body Position: Lying down

Hand Grip: Thumbs-Down

Parachute Position: On the floor

Parachute Motion: Taut

Directions: First have all of the children take off their shoes. Pretend that the parachute is a fresh layer of snow. Have the children hold onto the chute and keep it fairly taut. Have two to three children crawl onto the chute and lie on their backs. Then begin to make their angels by waving their arms and legs back and forth. When the angels are finished, the children should crawl off of the chute. Several more children should crawl onto the chute and make their snow angels. Continue until everyone has made a snow angel.

The Circle Time Book

by Liz and Dick Wilmes

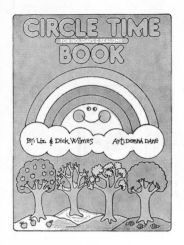

The Circle Time Book captures the spirit of seasons and holidays. The big book is filled with more than 400 circle time activities for the preschool classroom. Thirty-nine seasons and holidays are included.

A useful companion to **Everyday Circle Times.**

ISBN 0-943452-00-7, Building Blocks, 128 pages $8.95

Everyday Circle Times

by Liz and Dick Wilmes

Over 900 ideas for Circle Time. This is one of the most important and challenging periods in the children's day. Choose activities from 48 different units. Each unit is introduced with an opening activity, and expanded through language and active games, fingerplays, stores, recipes, books and more.

ISBN 0-943452-01-5, Building Blocks, 216 pages $12.95

Felt Board Fun

by Liz and Dick Wilmes

Make your felt board come alive. Discover how versatile it is as the children become involved with the wide range of activities designed to help them think creatively and learn basic concepts.

This unique book contains over 150 ideas with accompanying patterns.

ISBN 0-943452-02-3, Building Blocks, 224 pages $12.95

Imagination Stretchers

by Liz and Dick Wilmes

Have fun as you help your children learn to think creatively, use their past experiences, develop language, and enjoy sharing ideas. Choose from over 400 conversation starters designed to encourage each child to express his/her feelings, thoughts and opinions on a wide variety of topics.

ISBN 0-943452-04-X, Building Blocks, 88 pages $6.95

Parachute Play

by Liz and Dick Wilmes

Now a year-round approach to one of the most versatile pieces of large muscle equipment. Starting with the basic techniques, **Parachute Play** provides you with over one hundred activities to make your parachute or a large bed sheet come alive for the children in your group.

ISBN 0-943452-03-1, Building Blocks, 96 pages $7.95

Exploring Art

by Liz and Dick Wilmes

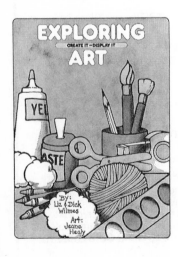

Create it — Display it — Enjoy it — the secret to enhancing your children's art experience. **Exploring Art** features a variety of easy art activities for each month. Every idea is coordinated with an introductory activity, a display suggestion, and extension activities for expanding art into the curriculum. Over 250 art ideas in all, along with more than 500 related activities.

ISBN 0-943452-05-8, Building Blocks, 256 pages $16.95

Everyday Bulletin Boards

by Liz Wilmes and Vohny Moehling

Everyday Bulletin Boards will help your classroom come alive with color, creativity, and charm. This book is a complete bulletin board resource, filled with easy and appropriate activities the children can do, plus an entire section of teacher-made boards with accompanying patterns. An absolute must for your library.

ISBN 0-943452-09-0, Building Blocks, 120 pages $8.95

Gifts, Cards, and Wraps

by Liz Wilmes and Dawn Zavodsky

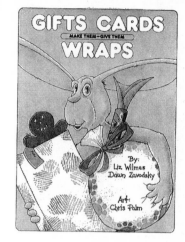

Help the children sparkle with the excitement of gift-giving. **Gifts, Cards, and Wraps** is filled with thoughtful gifts, unique wraps, and special cards which the children can make and give. Use the ideas for year 'round gift-giving. They're sure to bring smiles.

ISBN 0-943452-06-6, Building Blocks, 104 pages $7.95

Parent Programs and Open Houses

by Susan Spaete

Parent Programs and Open Houses is filled with a wide variety of year 'round presentations, pre-registration ideas, open houses, and end-of-the-year gatherings. All involve the children from the planning stages to the programs themselves. Try them. Everyone will have a good time.

ISBN 0-943452-08-2, Building Blocks, 152 pages $9.95

Classroom Parties

by Susan Spaete

Each party plan suggests decorations, trimmings, and snacks which the children can easily make to help set a festive mood. Choose from games, songs, art activities, stories, and other related experiences which will add to the excitement and fun.

ISBN 0-943452-07-4, Building Blocks, 120 pages $8.95